Looking at . . .

South Lancashire

MILLINER & HABERDASHER

LOUISA

"Spartina"

A "Dalesman" Paperback

Looking at
South Lancashire

40p.

Looking at
South Lancashire

by
"Spartina"

THE DALESMAN PUBLISHING COMPANY LTD.
Clapham, (Via Lancaster)
Yorkshire

1SBN: 0 85206 109 9

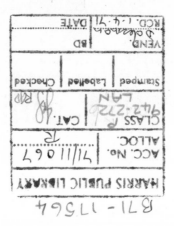
First Published 1971

© "Spartina" 1971

Printed by Galava Printing Co., Ltd.. Hallam Road, Nelson, Lancs.

Contents

"Spartina" is a group of four Lancashire authors, Dorothy Pilling, Mollie Thompson, Daphne Tibbitt and Diana Underwood. They would like to thank all those persons who have so willingly supplied information and without whose help this book would not have been possible. The front cover photograph of Lark Hill Place, Salford is by Salford Art Galleries and Museums and the map on the back cover is by Janet Ellerington. Illustrations in the text are by H. Pilling.

Introduction

IN these books, which we hope will be of as much interest to the resident as the visitor, we have tried to dispel the myth that Lancashire is the ugly sister of the North, dull and uninteresting. We hope you will be interested to read of ghosts and witches, the legends associated with them, and the fine abbeys, churches and mansions with which Lancashire abounds. Delve into the past at one of the many museums and examine unique collections of dolls, aircraft and railway engines; try some of the county dishes and see where they are made; or take part in some of the more unusual sports and hobbies or local customs. Take a lazy trip down one of the many canals, search for the wild life or go fishing. Explore the docks and harbours and watch the fishing fleet sail out to sea, following a channel taken by the Vikings many years ago. Lancashire holds many treasures, old and new. It is a county which gives a little of everything—sea and mountain, cities and small hamlets, and each has a place to explore.

1: A Short History of Lancashire

LANCASHIRE and its peoples have lived through many changes from the invasion of the Romans to the invasion of the Industrial Revolution. The county accepted each new influx of men and ideas and absorbed them into its pattern, and it is this pattern which can be rediscovered today in "Looking at Lancashire."

Roman conquest of Britain began in 43 A.D. and it was sixteen years later that the conquest of the North West began, the Romans crossing the Mersey at Latchford and proceeding across the Ribble. The tribe of Brigantes lived in Northern England and they were used by the Roman soldiers to build roads and the garrisons at Ribchester (Brenetennacum) and Manchester (Mancunium). Excavations have revealed a considerable number of Roman objects: inscribed altar stones, coins, jewelry and pottery. A bronze helmet was found at Ribchester in 1796, a bronze bust of Minerva at Warrington and the remains of an altar at Wigan.

When the Angles came into Lancashire from Yorkshire, Northumberland and Durham in about 570 A.D., some settled in the valleys of the Lune and Ribble until the 11th century. The population of Angles increased, names such as Wigan, Treales and Makerfield date back to this period. There have been a few Anglo-Saxon finds; coins at Little Crosby near Liverpool and at Heaton Moor near Lancaster. A chest containing ingots of silver and 10,000 silver coins was found at Cuerdale, near Preston in 1840, and was known as the "Cuerdale Hoard". Some of these coins were Danish and some were of the period of Alfred the Great and his son, Edward the Elder. The Danish invasion of Lancashire began with isolated raids, but evidence of settlement is shown in such names as Hulme, Davyhulme, Levenshulme, Oldham, Flixton and Urmston in the Manchester area. About 900 Norsemen settled in the county and the names Scales, Scarisbrick and Norbreck are Norse, while those of Goosnargh and Grimsargh are of half Irish-Norse descent. Norse crosses have been found at Whalley, Lancaster, Bolton, Winwick, Halton and Urswick. They consist of a circle between the arms of the cross, and are usually of stone and carved with snake and chain decorations. Norse tombs, known as hogsbacks, are to be found at Heysham and Bolton-le-Sands. Edward the Elder and

Aethelflaed, children of Alfred the Great, built forts at Thelwall and Runcorn, while the land between the Ribble and the Mersey was a royal domain until after the Norman Conquest. The Domesday Book states that at this time Lancashire was wooded, with scattered farmsteads and vast areas of rough grassland.

During the reign of William I, the county was administered by the King's cousin, Roger of Poitou, who chose Lancaster as the site for his castle. This was the beginning of Lancashire's close connection with the Royal family. In the 15th century the confiscated lands of the supporters of Lambert Simnel, pretender to the throne, were given to Lord Strange, son of the Earl of Derby. These gifts included estates in Wigan, Bury, Salford and Manchester, estates south of the Ribble and the Broughton estates in Furness and Cartmel, and thus the Derby family became the richest and most important in Lancashire. The Earldom of Derby has played a prominent part in the county throughout the centuries, King Henry VIII and Queen Elizabeth I having stayed at Knowsley Hall, home of the Earls of Derby.

In the reign of Elizabeth I, Lancashire was the strongest Catholic county, although Manchester and Bolton were strongholds of Puritanism. Religious belief was the deciding factor in the Civil War; in 1642 Lord Derby led the Royalists and some years later Cromwell marched down the Ribble valley and gained control of Preston. Later Lord Derby's army was defeated and he was taken prisoner, tried and executed in 1651. During Jacobite times there was dissension and plotting, the Lancashire Jacobites encouraging the Scottish Jacobites to invade England by way of Lancashire. This they did in 1715, but were defeated. The next attempt was in 1745 when Bonnie Prince Charlie with his troops came to Lancaster, Preston and Manchester, planning to march to London, but at Derby he abandoned the march and returned to Preston. In Tudor and Stuart times the population of Lancashire was small, but there were great industrial developments. By the 18th century more people were coming into the county, and with the Industrial Revolution the problem of poverty was rife. It was during this time that Lancashire's cotton industry came to the fore and her trade steadily increased. Mills, coal mines, factories and docks covered large areas. The opening of the Manchester Ship Canal in 1894, the construction of the East Lancashire road in the 1920s and the making of the Mersey Tunnel in 1934 greatly improved communications.

Lancashire with its industrial regions is one of the mainsprings of Britain's commerce. Manchester is the centre of the cotton industry and electrical engineering. St. Helens, largest producer of glass in the world, also has large chemical factories, copper foundries and cable works. Liverpool is one of the world's great trading centres with its docks, shipyards and airport.

Traditional Foods

THERE is an old Lancashire saying: "Trouble is naught, cost is all." The inhabitants of the county suffered hardship and poverty during the Industrial Revolution, and this was probably the reason for the traditional foods of Lancashire being cheap, appetising, nourishing, easily prepared and easily obtained. Most families, if fortunate enough to be in employment, were working in the mills, factories and local coal mines, and would buy food on the way home from work. The corner shop and small home-made bakeries were the source of many traditional foods.

Eccles Cakes were originally made in a small, family shop and became world famous. Bradburns Eccles Cakes were sent to all parts of the world. The cakes are round, consisting of a mixture of currants, sugar and chopped peel inside a short pastry case. The tops are dusted with fine sugar.

Lancashire Cheese is a popular and rich delicacy. It can be bought either mild or "tasty", the latter being of a strong flavour. In spite of competition from continental and fancy cheeses, Lancashire cheese is still a firm favourite and can be found in all the grocery shops and markets. Cheese and pickled onions are available in country inns throughout the county, while cheese and apple pie are traditional Lancashire fare which go well together.

Lancashire Hot Pot is an economical dish made from potatoes, onions and cheap cuts of lamb or mutton. This dish is left in the oven to cook slowly for many hours, and requires little attention. Traditionally it is cooked in a brown earthenware dish with a plate on top.

Manchester Pudding is a popular family pudding—light, nourishing and sweet. Alternate layers of apricot jam and thick egg custard are placed in a dish. The whites of eggs are whipped with castor sugar into a stiff mixture, and a few drops of vanilla essence are added. The meringue is then spread on top of the pudding. It looks and tastes delicious. There is a more substantial and filling recipe for Manchester pudding. The bottom of a pie dish is lined with pastry and is covered by a layer of jam. Breadcrumbs, milk flavoured with lemon peel, beaten eggs and sugar are mixed together and put on top of the jam. The pudding is then baked for about one hour; it is served cold sifted with sugar. Mrs. Beeton suggests adding three tablespoonfuls of brandy. Either of these puddings is appetizing and nourishing, even without the brandy, and to quote Mrs. Beeton "seasonable at any time."

Tripe.

Tripe is another popular dish in the area. Lancashire tripe is bleached and cooked and can be eaten cold as bought. Tripe and onions is made by cooking the tripe in milk and then adding a sauce from cooked onions, cornflour and milk. This is very nourishing and cheap. Tripe on a skewer used to be sold in Bolton at the fair every January 1st, together with black peas.

Trotters of pigs and the feet of sheep are boiled and skinned, cooked with onions and served with white sauce made from the stock, or eaten cold.

3:   Legends, Ghosts and Witches

Boggart Hole Clough, Blakeley

AT Blakeley, now on the outskirts of Manchester, there once stood a farm belonging to a farmer called George Cheetham. He and his family were tormented by a boggart, and a nearby dell was called the "Boggart Hole Clough." Whenever an amusing tale was told at the farm the boggart's shrill voice could be heard laughing loudly. One evening this laughter had again been heard and Robert, the youngest of the farmer's sons, demanded to see the boggart. No more laughter was heard, but that night Robert and his brother were dragged about their bed while the boggart laughed gleefully. The next morning the farmer on hearing the boys' story moved their bed to the cart house.

Now the boggart, with a room of his own, considered himself not just a visitor but a member of the family. His playful tricks increased, though sometimes he would be kind and churn the cream or clean the pans. In the farmhouse the stairs went up out of the kitchen and in one stair was a large knot-hole, said to be the boggart's peep hole. Immediately the shoe horn was thrown by an invisible hand at the head of the nearest child. Soon the boggart returned to his nightly tricks, clattering up and down stairs, throwing pots and pulling the curtains of the children's beds.

At last George Cheetham and his family could stand it no longer and they decided to move. The day arrived and the furniture had all been loaded onto a cart when a neighbour called. The farmer explained to his neighbour that because of the tiresome boggart they were moving. A little voice immediately piped up, "Aye neighbour, we're flitting." Wearily the farmer and his wife unpacked their furniture. From that time on, however, the boggart never annoyed the family again. Although the farm no longer remains, the nearby dell is now part of one of Manchester's parks and has been called Boggart Hall Clough. (See p. 27).

The Prior of Burscough

A N ancient legend is attached to Burscough Priory. It concerns one Michael de Pointinges, who was sent to the Priory seeking the whereabouts of a missing woman named Margaret de la Bech. Approaching the Priory, Michael met a woman who, seeming to know cf his mission, begged him to turn back. This Michael refused to do. On reaching the Priory he was shown to Prior Thomas who vehemently denied all knowledge of the missing woman.

On his return to Ormskirk, Michael met a man called Thomas le Clarke, who told him that although Margaret had been presumed drowned, her body had never been found. He had, however, heard strange noises coming from a barn, and on being offered money, he agreed to take Michael to the place. Taking servants and horses they rode to the barn about a mile from the Priory. Outside, a moaning noise could be heard which Michael recognised as the voice of the woman he had previously met. Her name was Isabel and she offered to show Michael her prisoner. Taking him to a damp cellar he found Margaret, now completely insane, having been brutally bound and tortured.

Carrying Margaret, Michael was making good his escape when an arrow, intended for him, killed Thomas le Clerke. Michael called to his servants, but it was too late and he too was killed. His servants rode off with his body and took Margaret to a safe place. The Prior was so in the favour cf the King that he was granted a most gracious pardon in the twenty-first year of the reign of King Edward III for his crimes against Margaret de la Bech and the murder of Michael de Pointinges and Thomas le Clerke. (See Burscough Priory, p. 33).

The Boggart of Clegg Hall

C LEGG Hall near Rochdale was the haunt of one of Lancashire's most famous boggarts. This was known as the Clegg Hall boggart, and tales of him are supposed to have begun after a terrible murder had been committed where Clegg Hall later stood. About the 13th or 14th century a wicked uncle murdered the two heirs of the house who were orphaned and had been left in his care. He threw them over the balcony and into the moat where they drowned. The house was said to be the haunt of a troubled spirit after the murder, even though the original house was pulled down.

About the year 1620, thirty years after the building of the new house on the site, signs of the presence of a boggart were still to be seen. The legend of Clegg Hall tells how one evening Nicholas Haworth and his sister Alice, owners of the Hall, were setting out to a marriage ball at Stubley. In the garden they met a beggar called Noman who gained food and lodging through fear. During the ball two strangers arrived and singled out Alice. Before her they performed conjuring tricks, till finally a mechanical bird gave her a message in its beak. The message told her to go to the haunted room at Clegg Hall the following night at midnight. This was where the boggart was supposed to live and where Noman stayed.

The following night Alice went alone to the haunted room. Suddenly the light she was carrying was blown out, she was seized and taken through passages to a cellar. Here she was left, only to discover she was surrounded by hoards of foreign coins. The man who had given her the note appeared and indicated that he loved her and would give her this money if she married him.

The next morning Alice was missed. Nicholas was told by Noman that she was held by the boggarts. He offered to try and exorcise the spirits, which he said were of the two murdered children, and return Alice. That night shrieks and rumblings were heard throughout the house. The next day Noman ordered a cockerel to be sacrificed, quartered and buried. Suddenly there was a tremendous explosion. Noman ran to the haunted room and returned with Alice in his arms.

It was later discovered that Noman, his son and a friend, had been making counterfeit money in the cellars of the house. The house was pulled down and destroyed, together with a large hoard of the counterfeit money. Noman, whose real name was Clegg, had hoped through fear to drive out Alice and her brother and take possession of his ancestor's home, Clegg Hall. Had his son not become infatuated with Alice his plan might well have succeeded. Although Noman used the legend of the boggart to explain the noises made in the cellars, it seems certain that a boggart did in fact exist at Clegg Hall.

The Eagle and Child

THE following legend concerns the origin of the crest of the eagle and child, famous in Lancashire. In the year 1343 Sir Thomas Lathom of Lathom married, and though twelve years passed by he had no heir, only a daughter, Isabel. In despair Sir Thomas was unfaithful, and as a result the daughter of a yeoman bore him a son. Sir Thomas formed a plan by which his wife would accept the child as their own. Nearby was an eagle's nest, and here the baby was taken and laid at the foot of the crag. The following morning as Sir Thomas and Lady Lathom walked they discovered the baby. Sir Thomas, feigning surprise, declared it was a gift from providence dropped by the eagle from the sky. The baby was taken home and baptised Oskatell, and Sir Thomas took an eagle for his crest.

Later Oskatell went to the Court of King Edward. There he was one of the knights, with Captain Stanley (later Sir John), who accepted a challenge from a number of French knights. His sister, Isabel, accompanied him to Winchester and there she was presented to the King, who made her brother Sir Oskatell de Lathom. Early the next morning Isabel received a love note from Sir John. Her father, not considering Sir John good enough for his daughter, turned over his wealth to Oskatell. Eventually Isabel eloped to Staffordshire and married Sir John Stanley. When he later died in Ireland she returned to live in Liverpool with their three children, two sons John and Thomas and a daughter.

Meanwhile Sir Thomas, now an old man, was suddenly conscience stricken. He placed all his estates in his daughter's hands, the manors of Irlam and Urmston being left to Sir Oskatell, who was also given the crest of the eagle. His rivals eventually took the present crest, the Eagle and Child, which the descendants of Sir John Stanley, the present Earls of Derby, continue to hold.

The crest of the eagle and child is found in many places in Lancashire, among these being the font at Ormskirk church—and a plaque bearing the crest at Childwall parish church. This plaque was probably presented to the church when the Stanley family became Lords of the Manor. (See page 33).

Miss Beswick of Manchester

MISS Beswick, a wealthy estate owner, lived on the outskirts of Manchester at her home "Birchen Bower" during the 18th century. She managed her estates well, until old age forced her to move from Bower House to a small cottage nearby. In 1475 Prince Charles, the Scottish Pretender, invaded England. Hearing of his advance into Lancashire, Miss Beswick hid her money and valuables in her old home. Relatives did their best to move into the house and find out where her wealth was hidden, but without success. "Birchen Bower" remained empty, save for the old lady's treasure.

Suddenly, Miss Beswick died, and in her will left the house to her medical attendant—Doctor White. The will also stipulated that Miss Beswick's body should not be buried, but embalmed and kept above ground. It was also required that every 21 years the body should be taken back to the old house and set in the granary for a period of one week. Some people thought that these strange requests arose from Miss Beswick's fear of being buried alive, but it was generally accepted that they were a way of keeping the old lady's curious relatives out of her old home.

The doctor however, complied with the will. Miss Beswick's body was coated in tar and wrapped in heavy bandages, leaving her face uncovered. With all her requests granted Miss Beswick's spirit should have rested in peace, but on many occasions the ghost of the old lady was seen around her old home. She would appear dressed in her black silk gown and lace cap, moving between the great barn and the horse pond, and often the barn would glow as if on fire.

For many years the embalmed body was kept in the doctor's own home. It was later removed to the museum of the Manchester Natural History Society. About 100 years after her death the society deemed Miss Beswick's body "undesirable", and she was buried on July 22nd, 1868, in Harpurhey cemetery. There is, however, a happy postscript to the story. The beginnings of the 19th century saw alterations to the old house at "Birchen Bower". It was renovated and made into several smaller homes for occupation by labourers. In one of the homes lived a poor handloom weaver, known as "Joe at Tamers", and concealed under the floorboards Joe found a hoard of gold wedges—part of Miss Beswick's hidden treasure.

Martin Mere and the Legend of Sir Lancelot

ONE of the earliest traditions of Lancashire concerns Sir Lancelot of the Lake. According to legend, Lancelot was the son of Ban, King of Benoit in Brittany. After fleeing from his enemies in France, King Ban died soon after reaching England. His Queen, Helen, while attempting to save her husband's life, left her baby son by the side of a lake called Martin Mere. When she returned she found her son with the nymph Vivian, the Mistress of Merlin, and as the Queen approached the nymph disappeared into the lake with the child.

At the age of 18 the boy was taken to the Court of King Arthur where he was knighted Lancelot of the Lake. The name is derived from "Lanc," the Celtic for spear, and "lot" meaning people, and is thought to have been the origin of Lancelot's shire or Lancashire. During many battles with the Knights of the Round Table against the Saxons, Lancelot heard tales of a treacherous Saxon giant whose castle was near Manchester. Lancelot set out to slay the giant, Tarquin, and free the captured knights held prisoner at the castle.

On reaching this place Lancelot met a beautiful maiden who warned him to flee for his life, but this Lancelot refused to do. The maiden then rode with him till they reached the castle, in front of which stood a tree laden with the weapons of the captured knights. Beneath hung a copper basin daring anyone to strike it and thus summon the giant. This Lancelot did and soon Tarquin appeared. Then the dual began and all day Lancelot and the giant Tarquin fought. During the battle Tarquin broke Lancelot's sword, but the maiden pointed to the tree, and Lancelot picked a broad sword from its branches, whereupon the fight continued. Eventually the swords of the two knights were somehow exchanged, and as the giant's sword possessed greater strength, Lancelot was able to kill him with his own sword.

Lancelot then determined to release the captured knights and the maiden showed him a secret horn which, when blown, would lower the drawbridge. A dwarf hidden inside the castle and armed with a mace, tried to kill Lancelot, but again the maiden saved his life by drawing him swiftly to one side. Lancelot then killed the dwarf with the giant's sword. Turning to the maiden he saw her suddenly change and vanish from sight, and he knew she was the nymph Vivian.

Lake Linius or Martin Mere is now cultivated. It lay between Formby and Ormskirk and was the largest inland lake. Holmeswood in this area is still said to be haunted by the ghosts of King Arthur's Court.

The Building of Rochdale Church

DURING the reign of William the Conqueror a Saxon named Gamel decided to build a church on the bank of the river Roach at Rochdale. The foundations were laid and all was ready for the building to begin. However, according to legend, that night the materials were moved to the top of a nearby hill—an inhuman feat.

Gamel was much displeased and a proclamation was read that the guilty parties would be punished. The frightened villagers decided that it was the work of the heathen gods worshipped by their forefathers whose altars were destroyed, and who were now taking their revenge. They gave a pledge to Gamel that the materials would be returned to their original site and a watch would be kept. The men were trying to decide how this should be done when an old woman named Cicely came up to them, mocking them for their cowardice. Now Cicely had a son, who it was said was the result of the old woman's illicit union with a pixie. The boy was dumb, but the old woman somehow understood his mumblings, and the people thought them both evil. Finally they offered to give the woman food and clothes if her son would keep watch that night. This she agreed upon.

The next morning the building had again been moved and the boy was missing. In great fear the men went to report to Gamel who this time threatened to imprison them and ordered the woman to be brought to him. Cicely wept and told Gamel she was bribed into letting her son keep watch. A man was summoned who claimed he had seen the devil at work the previous night moving the church. Gamel did not believe this story until a stranger reported seeing beings moving loads far in excess of those a normal man could move. Not knowing them to be devil's men he helped them and was rewarded with a silver ring.

Suddenly a shout was heard from the courtyard, and Cicely's son Uctred appeared. Seeing the silver ring he gave a hideous shout and placed it upon his finger. Immediately he appeared to grow more evil looking. Gamel ordered the guards to seize him, but the boy fled and when the guards reached the battlements only a thin wreath of smoke was seen in the valley. Gamel decided to build his church on the new site to appease the demons. This was done and 124 steps were carved to the top of the hill where the church still stands.

The Spectre Horseman

THIS legend is said to have taken place on the moors near Rivington Pike. Although the story may be difficult to believe in parts, nevertheless a spectre horseman was said to haunt the moors and certain of the events do seem to have occurred, although their explanation remains a mystery.

According to the legend, three men and their servants who had been grouse hunting on the moors were returning to a small inn for the night. A gathering storm seemed to lie directly in their path and they decided to shelter in a small nearby tower. One of the party called Norton seemed strangely disturbed by the storm. As they sheltered the dogs became uneasy, growling and barking. Horses hooves were heard approaching the tower and when Norton opened the door a horseman on a black horse was seen. Norton recognised the stranger as his uncle who had disappeared on the moors twelve years previously. As the stranger rode off Norton followed him. His friends were about to follow when one of the servants advised them not to. The horseman was the Spectre Horseman, a legendary figure in the district who was often seen.

Then the servant told of the night, exactly twelve years before, when his father had gone out poaching. He had watched for his father to return, but only the dogs came back alone and dirty. When his father returned much later he was in a very distressed state. He said he had been approached by a small man upon a large black horse who asked to be taken to The Two Lads, a pile of stones twelve feet high on the moor. The stones marked the place where two shepherd boys were said to have died. On reaching the place the horseman told him to lift up the stones, and he himself threw one high up in the air, at which the dogs ran home. Then his father remembered the tales of the Spectre Horseman, and where the stones had been there seemed to be a large black pit. At the approach of another stranger his father was knocked unconscious and when he awoke the stones were there as before. He went home never to return to the moor.

After listening to this story Norton's companions returned to the inn. Norton was not there so they set off towards the Two Lads to search for him. They found Norton at the foot of the pile of stones, apparently dead. He looked as though he had had a desperate struggle, and lay with hands clenched. They carefully lifted him up on to their horses and returned to the inn. A surgeon said Norton was exhausted both mentally and physically and he was unconscious for several weeks. When he recovered he said that his uncle, who had appeared that night as the Spectre Horseman, had made him promise to stay by the stones, and at midnight he would show him the purpose of his visit. His uncle returned saying he would possess Norton, and they fought. Norton was now convinced that his uncle was the stranger who had approached the devil and the servant's father twelve years before. To the day he died Norton was certain that his uncle was allowed to return only on the condition that the devil spirits which possessed him re-entered someone else. As this condition was not fulfilled when Norton refused to submit to him the Spectre Horseman was never seen again.

The Skull at Wardley Hall

WARDLEY Hall, which stands in the manor of Worsley, is the setting for one of Lancashire's most gruesome legends. This was the seat of the Downes family, and at the time of the story was inhabited by Maria Downes, her brother Harry, and their cousin Eleanor.

According to the legend, Maria and Eleanor were waiting at Wardley Hall one winter's night for the return of Harry from London. Fearing that he had become involved in a drunken brawl they were surprised when a messenger arrived from Manchester. He brought with him a wooden box which he said had come from London. Maria, feeling uneasy, refused to open the box and placed it in her room. During the night Maria imagined she saw a skull, grinning at her from the box.

The following day she put the box into an outhouse helped by her servant Dick and a maid called Betty. On leaving the outhouse a loud knocking was heard and the servants fled. Certain now that there was indeed something evil about the box, Maria went to open it alone. When she returned she claimed it contained nothing but straw. That night Dick, unable to sleep, saw Maria go into the outhouse and re-appear with something under her arm. This she buried in the garden.

All was well and the box forgotten until one day Maria, pale and trembling, told Eleanor to follow her. Going to the staircase she pointed to a mutilated skull in a niche in the wall where Harry, as a child, loved to play. At this Eleanor, who was in love with Harry, fell to the ground. She was put to bed but never recovered. Maria was then the only survivor of her family and she never married.

This is one of Lancashire's oldest legends, but it is thought there may be another explanation for the skull which is still preserved at Wardley Hall. Weight was added to this second theory when in 1792 the coffin of Roger Downes was opened in Wigan Parish Church. It was then revealed that although he had certainly been injured in a brawl, he did not in fact lose his head.

It is now believed that the skull was that of Ambrose Barlow, a Catholic priest. Father Ambrose was born at Barlow Hall, now a golf house, approximately 400 years ago. His family were Catholic nobility and were friends of the Downes family. Father Ambrose entered the priesthood at the age of 23. He was a pious man who did all he could to help the poor, providing them with meals whilst he ate the left-overs. When a decree went out banning the Catholic religion Father Ambrose was advised to flee. He continued to preach and was eventually betrayed by Protestants who wanted him arrested. On Easter Sunday 1641 he was arrested at Leigh while holding a service. His congregation begged him to escape, but he stood firm. He was taken to Lancaster to stand trial, found guilty and taken feet first on a hurdle to his place of execution, where he was hung, drawn and quartered. His remains were displayed as a warning to other Catholics, but his followers secretly removed his head which was taken to Wardley as a precious relic.

It is thought that the story of Harry Downes may have been invented to hide the real identity of the skull at the Hall at a time when Catholics were hounded unmercifully. Father Ambrose was created a Saint by Pope Paul VI in October, 1970. Wardley Hall is now the official residence of the Catholic Bishop of Salford.

4

Places of Interest

Knowsley Safari Park
*Route: B5194 which joins the A580 and the A57 east of Liverpool.
Open from July 1971; admission charge £1 per car.*

THE grounds of Knowsley Hall, the ancestral home of the Earl
of Derby, are to be opened from the beginning of July 1971 as a
Safari Park. The reserve will cover more than 360 acres of the
estate and visitors will be able to drive along approximately six miles
of road to view the many species of African wild life including the
largest captive elephant herd in the world. The park will consist of
four separate enclosures; the first for giraffes and zebras; the second
to be known as "the monkey jungle" for baboons and apes, and the
third for lions and cheetahs. It is hoped that eventually there will be
more than 40 lions within the reserve.

The fourth enclosure along the north boundary will contain
antelope, giraffe, deer, wildebeest and rhinoceros; it will *not* however be possible to drive through this section of the park owing to
the danger of attack from the rhinoceros. Other attractions will
include a restaurant to seat 500 people, a children's boating lake and
a separate picnic area. There will be a pet corner with many young
and tame animals and birds, and an African Craft shop. Ample
coach and car parking will be provided.

The Calder Stones, Liverpool.

THE six megaliths known as the Calder Stones now stand at the
main entrance to the Harthill greenhouses in Liverpool's Calderstones Park. However, their original location and purpose have been
the subject of much enquiry. They were first mentioned as a boundary
marker in 1568 when only three of the stones were uncovered, and
the earth mound under which they lay must have been the original
site. This mound was disturbed and most of it taken away at the end
of the 18th century and the archaeologists concerned found evidence
of burials in the form of urns containing fragments of human bone.
Unfortunately these burial remains have not survived. In 1845, Mr.
Joseph Walker of Calderstones House had the six stones moved to a
railed enclosure outside Calderstones Park.

On the scanty evidence now available it is impossible to be certain what kind of people erected the burial mound, but in 1954 a detailed study of the incised markings on the Stones reinforced the belief that they had formed part of a ''passage grave'' or communal burial chamber. Similar passage graves with carved stones have been found in Anglesey and Ireland dated approximately 2500 B.C. The Calder Stone markings include spirals, chevrons and human feet and this type of simple inscription has been noticed on other megaliths of the Stone Age and Bronze Age cultures discovered in many parts of the world.

The Mersey Tunnel

ALMOST a hundred years ago it was realised that some method had to be devised for linking Liverpool with her sister port, Birkenhead. The decision lay between a high level bridge and a tunnel construction, and eventually in 1922 the Merseyside Municipal Co-ordination Committee recommended a tunnel as being the best form of river crossing. H.R.H. Princess Mary performed the inauguration ceremony in December 1925 when, by turning compressed air into the drill at the working shaft, construction work officially began at George's Dock on the Liverpool side. A shaft was being driven from the opposite bank of the Mersey and by April 1928 the headings met under the middle of the river. July 1934 saw the opening of this, the largest sub-aqueous works in the world, by H.M. King George V.

It had been realised that the task of ventilating a tunnel system of this size would have to be given careful consideration, otherwise carbon monoxide gas emitted by vehicles would constitute a health hazard. Much data was collected and extensive experiments resulted in the adoption of a ventilation system known as the Upward Semi-Tranverse. This system consists of six ventilating stations, three on each side of the river. Fresh air is drawn into blowing fans through louvres fixed at roof level and projecting into the shafts connected with air ducts at road level. The exhaust outlets from the tunnel pass direct to ducts which terminate in the towers of the six ventilating stations.

The tunnel is 46 ft. 3 ins. in external diameter and 44 ft. in internal diameter. From sea level the roadways fall on a 1 in 30 gradient to its deepest point, and there are branch tunnels from the main artery serving dock traffic. When first built the length of tunnel roadway was over two miles, but with ever increasing traffic, plans for a second tunnel were drawn up and work began in 1966. The new tunnel will connect Wallasey with Liverpool and the construction work should be completed during 1970–71. In addition to this an improved system of approach roads will help considerably to ease the present traffic congestion.

The Parks of Liverpool

THE city of Liverpool is well endowed with parks and recreational areas. Originally these parklands formed part of the Perceval estates but, as Liverpool's merchants and shipowners increased in wealth, these wooded areas and rolling fields became the setting for handsomely proportioned private mansions. Now all this parkland belongs to the citizens of Liverpool, some 2,400 acres being distributed throughout the Liverpool area.

Harthill and Calderstones Park. At the entrance to Calderstones Park are the two ancient stone relics, the mysterious Calder Stones from which the park takes its name (see p. 20). Harthill is the site of the city's Botanic Gardens, first planted in 1803 and twice rebuilt since that time. The glasshouses contain a wide selection of plants ranging from the exotic orchids and rather terrifying flesh-eating plants to those of commercial value such as coffee, rubber and banana. The tree-backed parkland includes a boating lake, water garden, an open-air theatre and facilities for angling and bowling.

Clarke Gardens and Woolton Wood. In Clarke Gardens stands Allerton Hall, once the home of William Roscoe whose collection of paintings now hangs in the Walker Art Gallery. (See p. 47). The last family to live at Allerton were the Clarkes whose name the park now bears. Open grassland leads to Springwood or, in the opposite direction, to Camp Hill and from here a path leads into Woolton Wood. Two of the main attractions of this area are the children's zoo and aviaries in Clarke Gardens, and the Florentine garden with its floral clock, reached from Woolton Wood. Woodlands surround the Clarke Gardens region and among its inhabitants is a herd of Soya sheep native to the Atlantic island of St. Kilda.

For the fishing enthusiast facilities are available at Newsham, Stanley, Sefton, Calderstones, Greenbank and Walton Hall Parks. There is also ample provision made for golf and tennis. Model yacht lakes are provided in Newsham and Walton Hall Parks, and the boating lake in Sefton Park is also available for this purpose. During the summer months the list of shows, tournaments and general attractions is so comprehensive that it might be advisable for the visitor to obtain further information from: Director of Parks and Recreation, The Mansion House, Calderstones Park, Liverpool LI8 3JD.

Speke Hall, Liverpool. (National Trust)

Route: From Liverpool A562 to Hunt's Cross. Turn for Speke; join B5170. Admission: 12½p. Opening Times: April–September:—Weekdays: 10 a.m.–7 p.m. Sundays: 2 p.m.–7 p.m. (October–March:—Weekdays: 10 a.m.–5 p.m. Sundays: 2 p.m.–5 p.m.)

THERE has been a dwelling on this site since before 1066, and the Domesday Book records that the "Manor of Spec" was then the

Speke Hall, Liverpool

property of one "Uctred." This is thought to have been a sandstone house judging from the sandstone plinth on which the Tudor structure was erected. Subsequently the estate passed to many families, either by purchase or inheritance, until in 1490 it was acquired by Sir William Norreys. The oldest portions of Speke Hall date from this time. Succeeding generations of the Norreys family made many alterations and additions to the structure. The William Norreys at the time of the Civil War aligned himself with the king; as a result the entire estates were seized by the Parliamentarians in 1650. William soon renounced the Catholic Faith but to no avail, and not until 1662 were the estates returned to his son, Thomas.

The family fortunes declined steadily, the Hall drifted into disrepair, and in 1797 the property was sold to a West India merchant, Richard Watt. Watt spent vast sums of money on restoration and the wonderful condition of Speke Hall today is largely due to the care lavished upon it by him. The last member of the Watt family died in 1921 without issue, and eventually Speke Hall and grounds were given to the National Trust in 1942.

This beautiful hall, once moated but now surrounded by gardens and sweeping lawns, has its southern aspect overlooking the river Mersey. The courtyard contains two ancient yew trees, affectionately named "Adam and Eve," and known to be at least 400 years old. The interior of the hall has undergone many changes at the hands of its various owners, but some of the most outstanding features are the priest's hole and secret passage, the period furniture and the tapestry room with its fine example of Flemish work. This room is also known as the haunted chamber. Legend has it that one lady of the family, unable to face their financial ruin, killed her child by throwing it from one of these windows into the moat beneath, and then committed suicide. Her troubled spirit is said to haunt the scene of her pathetic crime.

The state bedroom derives its name from the long held belief that Charles I stayed at Speke Hall in 1630. If such was the case the King would have spent the night in the four poster bed which is exhibited in this room. One of the main features of the morning room is a fine overmantel in 18th century blue and white Dutch tiles, depicting the old Royal Palace at the Hague. Furnishings in this room also include a Regency chiming clock of about 1800, and an unusual clock which was the work of William Roskell, a famous Liverpool clock maker. The great parlour has a 16th century Italian stucco ceiling with an intricate design of grapes, flowers and nuts worked into it. An interesting feature of this room is the genealogical record carved into the overmantel; it shows a pictorial account of the lives, fortunes and deaths of three generations of the Norreys family.

Manchester Airport
On north side of A538.

SOUTH of the city, at Ringway, is Manchester's international airport. The roof terrace affords an excellent view of the airport, and special accommodation is provided for spectators. There is also a large restaurant overlooking the airfield. Arrangements for conducted tours of the airport buildings may be made by writing to the Airport Director, Manchester Airport, Manchester 22.

Chetham's Hospital School
Near the Cathedral, Manchester. School buildings:—Open: On application to the Governors. Library: Open to the general public.

THE Hospital School, situated in the heart of Manchester adjoining the Cathedral, is one of the oldest and best preserved examples in Britain of a medieval manor, dating back before 1420. About that time it became the College House of the Collegiate Church (now the Cathedral). When the College was dissolved in 1547 it was bought

**Statue in Manchester Cathedral of Humprey Chetham,
the founder of Chetham's Hospital School**

by the Earl of Derby. During Cromwellian times it was seized by the townsfolk and used as a garrison, store, prison and powder factory. The Great House, as it had become known, then lay idle for some years, until Humphrey Chetham, a wealthy banker and trader, left most of his fortune under his will of 1651 for a school for the sons of "honest, industrious and painful parents," together with a free library which was the first of its kind. In 1654 the Great House was taken over and opened soon afterwards as "Mr. Chetham's Hospital."

From that period came the Tudor uniform—long, belted bluecoat with brass buttons, yellow stockings, buckled shoes and pancake hat from which they became known, and are still known, as the "Bluecoat Boys." After World War II the school became an Independent Musical Grammar School and provided the statutory choristers for the Cathedral. By the autumn of 1969 it was Britain's first national school for young musicians. Throughout the years the library has continued to grow, visited by scholars from far and wide. Today it still contains some 65,000 books and MSS published from 1660 to the present day, including many valuable and rare volumes.

Manchester University—Jodrell Bank

On A535 between Chelford and Goostrey. Open: Daily during the summer from 2 p.m.–6 p.m. End October–Good Friday at week-ends 2 p.m.–5 p.m. (Christmas period excepted). Admission: Adults 17½p; Schoolchildren 10p.

THE Jodrell Bank telescopes are dedicated to pure astronomical research and are reserved, as far as possible, for work which no lesser instrument can do. The huge parabolic dishes dominate the landscape for miles around. The giant Mark 1 Radio Telescope took 3½ years to build, cost £700,000 and weighs 2,000 tons. It is claimed that 10,000 people could sit in comfort within the reflector bowl. The main elevating racks were taken from the gun turrets of the battleship "Royal Sovereign."

In May, 1966, the Department of Astronomy of Manchester University opened the Concourse Building to the public for the express purpose of explaining radio astronomy and the work of Jodrell Bank. The Main Hall holds display material giving in fairly simple terms an introduction to radio astronomy and, additionally, there are a number of models including a control desk from which visitors may drive a small 25 ft. radio telescope. Leading off from the Main Hall is a smaller exhibition gallery where details are given of the major experiments taking place in the research laboratories.

Manchester's Parks

MANCHESTER has many parks and open spaces, and can boast of having the first two public parks in the country, opened in 1846. During the summer a varied programme of entertainment is provided with open-air plays, variety shows and concerts. Children's shows, visiting fairs and circuses, sheepdog trials and horse shows also take place.

Heaton Park has an 18 hole golf course, pitch and put and a large boating lake. Near the Hall is a pets' corner and the park also contains a herd of Highland Cattle and a small flock of St. Kilda sheep. (See p. 48, Heaton Hall).

Wythenshawe Park, the most beautiful of the parks, contains the old Hall dating from the 1300s. A sports pavilion and a running track are part of the amenities, together with a stud of ponies especially for children's rides. (See p. 28, Wythenshawe Hall).

Alexandra Park is one of the older parks and is well known for a collection of cacti and succulent plants, said to be one of the largest in the country.

Boggart Hole Clough is an unusual name for a park. A boggart in the local dialect is an evil spirit, the full name meaning "den of the haunted spirit." The Clough is a mile in length with tree-clad slopes and valleys. Fishing facilities and a boating lake are available. (See p. 11).

Platt Fields contains the Shakespeare Garden where the herbs and flowers mentioned in his plays are grown. The park also contains part of an earth-working known as Nico Ditch, believed to date from Anglo-Saxon times. Here also is the Gallery of English Costume. (See p. 50).

The John Rylands Library
Deansgate, Manchester

THE Library was founded by Mrs. Rylands in memory of her husband; started in 1890 it took ten years to build and is considered to be one of the finest examples of neo-Gothic architecture in Europe. It opened for readers on January 1st, 1900. In the printed book department there are over 3,000 incunabula from the leading continental and English presses, including the earliest dated Western print, the "St. Christopher" of 1423; an impressive array of Bibles and valuable editions of English and foreign classics from the 16th century onwards. The manuscript department contains records on clay, bark, bamboo, papyrus parchment, paper and other materials representing over 50 different languages and cultures from the 3rd millennium B.C. onwards. There are superb examples of Eastern and Western calligraphy and illumination, and many unique and rare texts, including the oldest manuscript of the New Testament (the St. John fragment, c. 100–150). The Library's medieval jewelled bindings rank third among the world's collections.

Manchester Town Hall
Albert Square, Manchester. Permission to view can be obtained from the Town Hall Superintendent.

COMPLETED in 1877, the building is of Gothic style constructed of brick cased in sandstone. The most imposing aspect is seen from Albert Square, with the main frontage and clock tower. Over the main door is a statue of St. George, above which on the second floor are Henry III and Queen Elizabeth I. At the apex of the main door gable is a statue of the Roman General, Agricola, whose legions conquered the district.

Eight steps lead from the main entrance hall into the sculpture hall, a place of unusual design containing many statues and busts of persons connected with the City of Manchester. The groined roof of Bath stone is supported by pairs of detached granite shafts resting on granite bases. The first floor is probably the most interesting as it accommodates both the Large Hall and the Lord Mayor's state-rooms. The large hall, some 100 ft. long and 50 ft. wide, has a magnificent panelled ceiling bearing the arms of those countries and towns having business connections with the city, and also those of the royal family and the Duchy of Lancaster. The walls are decorated with 12 mural paintings by Ford Maddox Brown.

The clock tower is 281 ft. 6 ins. high, and entrance to the bell chamber, the clock mechanism and the great hour bell is obtained from the third floor by means of a circular staircase built into one of the angle turrets of the tower. The bell chamber contains 23 bells with a total weight of $12\frac{1}{2}$ tons. Thirteen of the bells form a ringing peal which, together with the remaining ten bells, are used in connection with the carillon. In the tower room on the first floor, and in the entrance hall, the roof has a large circular panel through which the bells can be lowered for repair or replacement. The clock dials are 16 feet in diameter, the minute hands are 10 feet long and the hour hands 6 feet long. The hours are marked by fleur-de-lis instead of figures. Above three of the clock dials is the inscription "Teach us to number our days" taken from Psalm 60, verse 12.

Wythenshawe Hall, Northenden

For Wythenshawe Park and Hall, leave Manchester on A56, in Sale, Gatley, Cheadle direction. Opening Times: Monday–Saturday: 10 a.m.–7.45 p.m. Sunday: 2 p.m.–7.45 p.m.

THE name of Tatton is well known as being that of an old established Cheshire family. They once owned large estates in Cheshire which overlapped into the areas now within the Manchester boundary. Wythenshawe Hall is known to have been continuously in the possession of some branch of the Tatton family from 1370 until 1926, when it was bought by Lord Simon of Wythenshawe and opened to the public. The present Hall stands on the site of an earlier building, and the oldest portion now remaining is the central block built during the reign of Henry VIII. The old house was originally surrounded by a moat but this was necessarily removed as later additions were made in Elizabethan, Jacobean and Georgian times.

Much of this early structure is now hidden as a result of extensive alterations carried out in the latter part of the 19th century. However, some of the old panelling was incorporated in the redecoration of the main rooms prior to their being opened to the public. The most dramatic period of Wythenshawe Hall's history was undoubtedly during the Civil War. Robert Tatton fought on the side of the Royalists and the Hall was under siege for eighteen months before its final surrender to the Parliamentarians.

Visitors are shown damaged panelling in the drawing-room and cannon balls exhibited in the dining-room. There are also supposed to have been several skeletons dug up in the grounds in the 18th century; this may or may not be true, for there is no documentary evidence to support the claim. The furnishings exhibited in the

Wythenshawe Hall, Northenden

ground floor and first floor rooms are mainly of the 17th century, with a notable display of pictures and ceramics in the dining room. Among the chief exhibits in the first floor front bedroom is a fine old four poster bed dated 1619. The walls of the ante-room, staircase and landing are hung with pictures principally of the 16th and 17th centuries.

Ordsall Hall, Salford

Route: Preston/Chorley A6 through to Salford. The Museum's opening is scheduled for 1971–72.

THE site of Ordsall is first mentioned in 1177 when it was in the possession of the de Poitou family. The influence of the Norman

Ordsall Hall, Salford

Conquest can also be seen in the names de Ferrers and de Hulton, successive owners of this Manor House which was strategically placed near a ford over the river Irwell. Seeing the Hall today, surrounded by factories and houses, it is difficult to visualise the large stretches of arable land which then existed. Being adjacent to the river, these lands around Ordsall were fertile at a time when the wealth of any family depended upon their farm lands.

Records show that there were three dozen manor houses within a five mile radius, and inter-marriage and feuds between the owners of Ordsall and other families in the area show the pattern of social life in those times. In 1335 Sir John Radclyffe inherited the property and it is interesting to note that, as a result of his trade associations with Flanders, a number of Flemish weavers and other craftsmen settled in Salford. Possibly this marked the beginning of the industrial life of the district. For the next 300 years descendants of John

Radclyffe owned Ordsall, during which time the family history shows their participation in the larger field of national history. Radclyffe sons fought at Agincourt, during the Wars of the Roses, and helped to supress Perkin Warbeck's invasion from Scotland. Two Radclyffe daughters and one cousin went to Court as maids-of-honour to Elizabeth I.

During the Tudor period the Radclyffe family had considerable wealth as evidenced by inventories of jewellery, clothes, cattle and sheep, and by the fact that in 1590 they "owned their own coach," apparently the first in Lancashire. Their connection with Court life in London must however have involved them in much expense, and gradually the Royalist family declined both in wealth and importance until, by the time of the Civil War, its ruin was complete. In 1654 Ordsall Hall passed out of their hands, being owned for periods of short duration by various families culminating in the Egertons. In 1896 Earl Egerton of Tatton converted the Hall into a clergy training school, later to be used as Rectory of St. Cyprions. The Hall was bought by Salford Corporation in 1959 and is now in process of restoration and adaptation as a Museum. A large collection of museum exhibits is being transferred to Ordsall in readiness for its opening to the public, either in 1971 or 1972.

5

Churches

Ashton-Under-Lyne: Church of St. Michael and All Angels
On A635 East of Manchester.

THE first church was built on the site in Anglo-Saxon times. Much restoration and re-building has taken place over the years, the most notable being that of 1400–58 when the church was re-built in stone by John Huntingdon, rector from 1400–22 and again from 1425–58. The greatest treasure of the church is the beautiful medieval stained glass preserved in many of the windows; it is considered one of the most important antiquities of the period. The windows in the south aisle show the life story of St. Helen, who some say was the daughter of Old King Cole (Coyl in the glass) of the nursery rhyme. The other glass memorials in this aisle are of the Assheton family, 1428–1516.

On the north sanctuary wall can be seen four sheets of metal on which the ten Commandments, the Lord's Prayer and the Creed are painted. These sheets are only to be found in older churches, as they were ordered to be put up during the Reformation. The centre aisle contains, halfway down its length, the 18th century three-decker pulpit; at the foot of the steps is a finely carved angel probably dating from the 17th century. Also to be seen here is a chained bible of 1593. In the churchwarden's pew is an old Book of Common Prayer, containing services commemorating the anniversary of the execution of Charles I and the order of service for Gunpowder, Treason and Plot, among many others. The roof of the chancel and nave is delicately carved, and although plastered over is similar to the roof in Manchester Cathedral, which was also designed by John Huntingdon. Below the bell tower is a charities board giving details of gifts made to the poor of the parish. On the opposite wall are the "pigeon holes" that used to contain 2-lb. loaves of bread for the needy.

Billinge: Church of St. Aidans
On the road from St. Helens to Wigan.

ABOUT 1534 the first small chapel was built on the hill top at Billinge, although it was probably never consecrated, there being no trace of any dedication. It must have been poorly furnished, as when visited by the King's Commissioners in 1552 they found little to plunder. It was re-furnished and again stripped in the reign of Queen Mary in 1553, the windows being broken and the building turned into a barn for the storage of grain and hay. In 1718 James Scarsbricke gave a sum of money in order that the chapel could be re-built. The oak panelling and the altar table, now standing under the war memorial, date from this time, as does the lovely brass candelabrum.

Restorations in 1907 proved that the present church was built on a much earlier chapel. A pleasing oblong building of excellent proportions and having a rounded apse, it has classic Doric columns supporting a long stone roof. The walls and ceiling are plastered, the latter being barrel vaulted over the nave. The windows have some unusual Gothic tracery and contain some rich blue Victorian glass. Beneath the record board is a tiny convex brass plate to James Scarsbricke, dated 1721. Externally, notice the urns set out along the embattled parapet and the huge bell in the cupola.

Burscough Priory
Abbey Lane, just off A59 Ormskirk Road.

THE Priory was founded for the Black Canons, an Augustinian Order, in 1190 and was so richly endowed that it became one of the most important religious houses in Lancashire. In 1296 there were a prior and six canons, and by 1536 at the dissolution there were a prior, five monks and forty dependants. Extensive excavations have provided a picture of the Priory as it was—a church with transepts, central tower and north aisle, chancel and chapels, a chapter house, a hospital for lepers and probably an almonary. All that now remains are the two pillars or piers of the central north arch of the church which supported the tower, together with a portion of the north wall of the chancel containing one side of a window. At the bottom of this pier is a canopied recess, in an excellent state of preservation, where the piscina originally stood and through which the water was thrown away after the rinsing of the chalice. The great tenor bell which once hung in the tower is now in Ormskirk church. (See p. 40).

Childwall, Liverpool: Church of All Saints
Near B5171.

THE first reference to Childwall is to be found in the Domesday Book of 1086. It is thought that the original dedication of the church was to St. Peter, as it is referred to as such in a 14th century document. A church was probably built on the site in Saxon times as fragments of carving can be seen on a stone in the west wall of the porch. The stone, thought to be the lid of a child's coffin, has a rough cross with barbs half way up the stem carved on it.

The present building dates from the 14th century, although many alterations and additions have been made. The church is built on the side of a hill, and originally the floor sloped with the fall of the land, there being three or four steps down to the chancel. In 1851 the floor of the chancel was raised three feet; this explains why the 14th century piscina is now at floor level. The ground outside the church has also been raised at some time, as can be seen at the porch entrance where there are now four steps down. The lepers' window just outside the porch is now almost below ground level instead of being above it.

The windows on the north and south of the chancel are also 14th century, as is the wall immediately behind the choir pews and the priest's door in the south wall, still in use to-day. Notice the carved acorns on the choir stalls and in other places in the church; ancient superstition said that they prevented evil spirits from entering the building. Acorns are often seen in windows. Near the porch stands the old churchwarden's pew of 1722. A recess has been cut in the nine foot thick tower wall to house the sandstone font which dates from 1622.

The Norris chapel on the south side of the church is known to have existed in 1484, and was then owned by Thomas Norris of Speke Hall. In one of the alcoves in the south aisle may be seen the brass to Henry Norris and his wife Clemence, dated 1524 and in an excellent state of preservation. Henry is wearing armour with spurs, sword and dagger; his wife wears a simple dress with an ornamental girdle and a cloak. The exquisitely carved bench end from the chapel now stands beside the lectern in the nave.

In another recess is an interesting wood carving of the eagle and child motif, seen incorporated in the arms of the Stanley family, the Earls of Derby (see the legend of the Eagle and Child p. 13). Probably the carving was presented to the church when the Stanley family became Lords of the Manor of Childwall in 1473. The tower, originally built in the 14th century, contains five bells, the oldest two dating from 1517.

Flixton: Church of St. Michael
Off A57 West of Urmston.

THERE was probably a church on this site before the Normans came to Lancashire in 1066. Of the Norman church all that remains is the east wall of the chancel; above the window on the outside of this wall is a carving of this period. The first noted rector of the church was Henry de Torboc, a monk from Burscough Priory, in 1198. In the baptistry can be seen an old oak desk, which from 1603 contained the registers of the church started by command of

Queen Elizabeth I in 1570. The chest has three locks, one for the minister and one for each of the churchwardens.

Near the south door can be seen the brass memorial to Richard Radcliffe, dated 1602. Here also can be seen the boards recording gifts to the poor. The tower originally built in 1500 contained two bells and in the 17th century two more were added. The sundial by the south porch was erected in 1772. Of interest are the verses on many of the older flagstones, the earliest of which is dated 1669. Look for those of the fiddler, the blacksmith and the mariner; also that of the wife of Ensign Ewart, who captured the French standard at the battle of Waterloo.

Halsall, Near Ormskirk: Church of St. Cuthbert
On A567 Southport–Liverpool Road.

STANDING on rising ground in the middle of the small village of Halsall, this very attractive church bears a charter dating from 1191 recording the grant of land "to God and St. Cuthbert of Halsall." The original church was probably Norman, and in 1290 the first major alterations were recorded when the lofty columns and beautifully moulded arches were added. The years 1340–50 saw the erection of the fine chancel, addition of the south aisle and the building of the tower and the fine steeply pitched roofs.

In the chancel, above the great east window, is the hand held up in benediction forming the apex of the hood mould. The magnificent 14th century doorway on the north wall, having three continuous moulded orders and the original door, should not be missed. The rich carving of the choir stalls and misericords is worthy of note. On the north wall of the chancel is the fragment of a brass showing a heraldic design and bearing an inscription, now badly broken, to Henry Halsall, dated 1589.

Externally the buttresses and pinnacles of the chancel are exceptional as are the many and interesting gargoyles. The numerous treasures of this delightful church can only be appreciated by a visit; before leaving be sure to see the remains of the 14th century priest's house lying in the north-east of the church.

Huyton: Church of St. Michael
East of Liverpool on the A5080.

THE original date of the church is unknown, the first mention being in the Domesday Book of 1086. There was certainly a Saxon church on the site, as has been proved by the finding of the capital of a small column, carved with four male heads each wearing a helmet as found in Saxon pictures. The south porch contains some interesting 15th century carvings. In the new baptistry is an ancient font which was buried for centuries below the floor. Made of red sandstone with beautifully sculptured designs and containing the original lead lining, it is believed to have been made in about the 8th or 9th century. A second font, probably early 16th century, is also to be seen.

The oak chancel screen is beautifully carved and dates from about 1460. The unusual credence table is thought to have been brought from the Netherlands in 1850. The southern arcade of the nave is 14th century, and in the south side of the chancel is a small 15th century priest's door. At the east end of the south aisle is a defaced and damaged effigy, made in alabaster, which probably dates from 1300. The tower, 13th–15th century, is decorated with pinnacles, battlements and gargoyles, each pinnacle having a metal wind vane in the form of a banner.

Liverpool Cathedral

THE foundation stone of the new Liverpool Cathedral, designed by Sir Giles Scott and G. F. Bodley, was laid on July 19th, 1904, and the building was consecrated on July 19th, 1924. The Cathedral, the largest in England, is still not complete, the third bay of the nave and the main entrance being under construction. Only a brief outline of this magnificent cathedral can be given here, omitting details of the rich carving or beautiful stained glass windows.

The nave is partially closed at the eastern end by the nave bridge, so that the vastness of the building cannot immediately be seen. The nave windows depict on the north side English musicians, hymn writers and scholars, and on the south side bishops, parsons and laymen. Beyond the nave bridge is the western transept, part of which forms the baptistry. The font, beneath an elaborately carved canopy, is of French marble and the twelve sides are each carved with the figure of an apostle. Above the entrance is a panel showing Christ calling the little children.

The central section, including the under tower, contains some of the most beautiful glass in the cathedral. Beyond this is the eastern transept, part of which forms the war memorial chapel. Beneath the entrance arch to the chapel stands the cenotaph containing the roll of honour, and hanging above the galleries on either side are 26 Colours, 23 of which belong to the various battalions of the King's Regiment (Liverpool). Beyond the eastern transept is the chancel consisting of three bays containing the choir stalls, the bishop's throne and clergy seats, and behind bronze communion rails the sanctuary. The altar is of panelled oak flanked on either side by marble sedilia. Behind the sanctuary is the great east or Te Deum window.

At the northern end of the ambulatory is the chapter house and at the southern end the Lady Chapel. The windows of the chapel depict women saints, and there is a memorial tablet to Liverpool

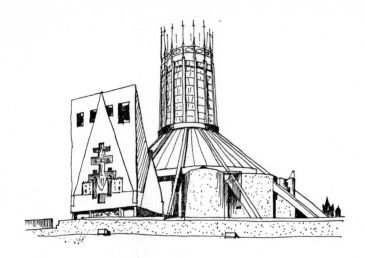

The Metropolital Cathedral, Liverpool

nurses who died in the First World War. A most beautiful reredos shows the Nativity above the baptism of Christ, and on either side the adoration of the shepherds. Above the vestry on the west side of the baptistry is the Radcliffe Library, containing many old and valuable books and manuscripts.

The Metropolitan Cathedral of Christ the King, Liverpool

IN 1928 Archbishop Richard Downey appointed Sir Edwin Lutyens as architect to design the new Liverpool Cathedral. Work began on the crypt which was finished at the outbreak of the last war, but by 1953 the estimated cost had risen from £3,000,000 to £27,000,000. This cost proved to be prohibitive. In 1959 a competition for a new design was held which would incorporate the existing crypt. From 300 entrants the design of Sir Frederick Gibberd was chosen and work commenced in October, 1962. The cathedral was consecrated on May 14th, 1967.

Modern in design, it is built to a circular plan, enabling 2,000 people to worship no further than 80 feet from the sanctuary steps. The high altar, in the centre of the cathedral, is a rectangular piece of white marble from Yugoslavia, and immediately behind is the choir. The pinnacled lantern tower above, in the shape of a crown, marks both internally and externally the high altar. The tower, weighing over 2,000 tons, depicts in an abstract design of stained glass the Blessed Trinity. Round the perimeter of the cathedral are ten chapels, separated by walls of coloured glass and each different in design and size. The most important is the Chapel of the Blessed Sacrament. This is lit by two triangular windows and the altar has a canopy faced in Portland stone. The tabernacle is richly decorated and surmounted by a large painted reredos.

One of the most important parts of the cathedral is the baptistry. This is a circular building and is entered through an opening into the nave enclosed by bronze gates, the lock of which is carved with the coat of arms of Liverpool. The font is of white marble with a dull silver cover. In the east tower is the gift to the Cathedral of Pope Paul VI, a bronze Holy Water stoup. Around the bowl are carvings of incidents in the life of Christ connected with water. Among other items of special interest is the Pruden Chalice. This is made from gold wedding rings bequeathed to the cathedral by Lancashire Catholics.

Manchester Cathedral

ALTHOUGH there was probably a Saxon church on the site of the present cathedral, little is known of it, the only clue being the "Angel Stone" found in the foundations and now kept on the north side of the chancel arch. In 1598 Thomas de la Warre gave his manor house to be the home of a collegiate body of priests and lay clerks, later to become Chetham's Hospital, and obtained a licence from Henry V for the building of a collegiate church. The original charter hangs in the cathedral.

Construction of the church as it is known today began in 1422 and the building was dedicated to St. Mary, St. Denys and St. George. The first rector was John Huntingdon who was until then rector of Ashton-under-Lyne, and it was he who built the choir and the aisles on either side. The work was continued by Ralph Langley and later by James Stanley, son of the first Earl of Derby. They built the nave and aisles, the octagonal chapter house with its impressive entrance, and the lofty clerestory windows. By this time, about 1500, many chantry chapels were being built round the aisles, thereby almost doubling the width of the church. During the last century all the remaining screens and partitions have been removed, making the nave one of the widest of any British cathedral—114 feet.

Throughout the cathedral the exquisite carving cannot fail to impress the visitor, much of it surviving from medieval times. The screen to the Lady chapel and the rood screen to the choir are surpassed only by the carvings in the choir, most of which date from 1508. The misericords—tip-up seats—of the choir stalls have carvings of many medieval stories and legends. The beautiful roof of the choir, designed by John Huntingdon, is divided into panels, each filled with rich tracery and with foliated bosses marking the intersections. The Regimental chapel on the north-east side of the choir, and of the same length, was built in thanksgiving for the safe return of Sir John Stanley from the battle of Flodden Field in 1513. It was serverely damaged during the air-raids of the Second World War, but has now been completely restored.

Although much of the beauty of the cathedral may have been destroyed through the centuries, the air of spaciousness and grace remains, with a "forest of pillars and arches of soft red stone." The skill of the craftsman can still be seen in the lovely roof of the nave and delicate fan vaulting in the west tower. Every window was blown out during the blitz, the Lady Chapel was completely destroyed and much of the carving damaged.

The cathedral contains many memorials, the finest of which must be the brass of John Huntingdon dated 1458. His hands raised in prayer, he wears choir habit, surplice and almuce (permission is never refused to those wishing to take brass rubbings). Also of note is the brass of about 1460 of Lady Margaret Byron, wife of the Steward of the College of Manchester; she wears a plain dress gathered in at the waist and a cloak fastened with a chord. Although badly mutilated the brass of James Stanley, Warden of Manchester, 1515 is still distinguishable. He is wearing a richly jewelled mitre, a short figured robe enriched with a foliated pattern and tasselled gloves over which he has many rings. In his left hand he carries a pastrol staff.

Middleton: Church of St. Leonard
On the A664 Manchester to Rochdale Road.

THE first church was built on this site in the 12th century; in the 15th century this was pulled down and completely rebuilt as a gift from Thomas Langley, Bishop of Durham. The only parts of the church remaining from the rebuilding of 1406 are the tower, the beautiful south porch, parts of the walls and the line of the south arcading. Further rebuilding took place between 1515–24 at the instigation of Richard Assheton, and only a few alterations and additions have been made since then.

The south porch, probably the finest of the period, still shows the rich and intricate carving that would have been in the 12th century church. The door leading to the south aisle is the original, and still has the drawbar which can be let into the thickness of the wall. To the east, leading into the Assheton chapel, is a doorway unlike anything else in the church; it is probably the priest's doorway from the 15th century building, and the window above could be of the same period. The western arch is all that remains from the 12th century church, and leads into the tower. The Hopwood pew of 1524 is a good example of a Jacobean box-pew, and occupying the width of the nave is a very fine 16th century screen. Some old carvings are to be seen in the choir stalls, all of which are misericords. A quaint feature is the snuff box built into the bench end of the north stalls.

All through the church there are reminders of the association with the Assheton family, one of the most striking being the Flodden window. Probably dated about 1520, it shows Sir Richard Assheton, his wife and chaplain together with sixteen archers. Although moved from its original position, the line of archers can be clearly seen, kneeling in prayer. Each is dressed in blue with a sheaf of arrows on his back, a long bow over his shoulder, and above his bow his name is inscribed.

The five Assheton brasses, which are some of the finest in the county, are now within the communion rails and are covered with a carpet. Dating from the 16th and 17th centuries they show:

1. Edward Assheton, rector of the church 1492–1522. The brass is as clear as when it was laid, and shows a graceful figure wearing church vestments and carrying a chalice. 1522.

2. Alice, sister of Edmund and Richard, shown with two of her three husbands, one on either side, both being knights dressed in armour. 1529.

3. Richard Assheton and his wife Elizabeth in Jacobean dress, with large ruffs. Below the father are shown his five sons and a baby; below the mother their two daughters wearing farthingales and ruffs. 1618.

4. Sir Richard Assheton and his wife Isobella. This brass also shows the family arms. Sir Richard, known as the Black Knight, is shown in armour. Beneath their parents are shown seven sons and six daughters. 1507.

5. Major General Ralph Assheton, Commander of the Parliamentary forces of the Civil War, and his wife Elizabeth. Sir Ralph wears full armour, as do his three sons. Elizabeth is shown in a dress with a pointed bodice, cap and veiling. Her three daughters are similarly dressed, with fans and feathers. 1650.

Permission to see the brasses should be obtained from the rector or the verger.

Ormskirk: Church of St. Peter and St. Paul
On A59 Liverpool–Preston Road.

THIS is a unique and interesting church with Saxon foundation having both a tower and a steeple. The small tower, probably dating from the late 14th or early 15th centuries is square but changes to octagonal and is finished with a tall slim spire. The massive west tower was added in 1550, and has corner stepped buttresses, battlements and pinnacles, and is said to be built of masonry from Burscough Priory. The ancient bells were also from the priory. On the external east side of the 12th century chancel is an ancient sculpture, possibly Anglo-Saxon, and there is evidence

St. Leonard's Church, Middleton

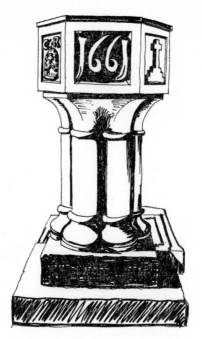

Font in Ormskirk parish church

of Norman work in the north window of the chancel. In the porch are the pews provided for the dog-whippers, and above the entrance can be seen a 17th century sundial. The font, dated 1661, was given to the church by the Countess of Derby and bears the Stanley insignia of the eagle and child. An hour-glass is fixed to the side of the bowl.

To the west of the chancel is the royal chapel, with the royal arms shown on the apex of the first arch. It was here that Henry VII came when on a visit to his stepfather, the Earl of Derby, at Lathom House. The Derby chapel, built in 1572 by the third earl, contains some alabaster monuments thought to be of the Earl of Derby and his two wives, the second being Lady Margaret, mother of Henry VII. The monument was moved from Burscough Priory where they had previously been buried.

The Scarisbrick chapel, separated from the Derby chapel by an oak screen, contains a fine life size brass, over five feet, of a member of the family. It depicts a knight in full armour, his feet resting on a lion couchant. He wears a sword, but unfortunately both the head

of the lion and the hilt of the sword are missing. The brass dates
from the late 15th century.

Sefton: Church of St. Helen
On B5422 7 miles North of Liverpool.

ONLY a little of this interesting and beautiful church can be
mentioned here. The original church was of the Decorated and
Norman period, built on the site of the present chancel about 1170.
Successive additions were made until 1540. The south porch has an
original fine oak ceiling; the door also is original and is hung on
fleur-de-lis hinges. At the west end of the church is the dog-
whipper's pew with curiously carved ends. The church guide states:
"It was the office of the dog-whipper to keep out any dogs that may
have followed their masters to church, and to arouse the sleepy
during the sermon."

The belfry is probably early 14th century with beautiful windows.
There are eight bells, two dated 1601 and two 1588. It is possible to
obtain access to the tower, and on ascending, notice the 13th century
coffin lid forming the ceiling of one of the tower turrets. It is a
fragment of exquisite medieval stone carving, and can also be seen
from below by mounting the stone staircase of the turret.

Most of the wonderful carving to be found in the church dates
from the 16th century and the richly carved caroline pulpit in the
nave was made in 1635. In the sanctuary there is much of note
including a stone at the side of the sedilia on which, it is said, the
priest once sharpened the arrows brought to be blessed before battle.
The stone on top of the steps dates from about 1170 and is probably
the oldest in the church.

The Molyneux chapel contains some interesting brasses. Between
the rail of the chapel and the pew is one of 1548 showing Sir William
Molyneux, Knight, and his two wives, Jane and Elizabeth. The
armour worn by Sir William is unusual for the period, and has given
rise to much speculation. The other brass in the chapel is that of
Sir Richard Molyneux, also with two wives, dating from 1568. The
Lady chapel contains two unique effigies. The one wearing plate
armour is probably 1330, and the other is about 1286. They are
said to be the best medieval monuments in Lancashire.

Points to note outside the church include the 14th century buttress
on the north side of the tower, the base of the old village cross and
nearby the old sundial. In the field opposite the church is the moat
and the scanty remains of Sefton Manor House. A short distance
down Lunt Road a flat stone commemorates St. Helen's well, said
to have held healing properties, and later used as a wishing well.

Winwick: Church of St. Oswald
On A49 North of Warrington.

PROBABLY the third church to stand on this site, the present
building dates from 1358. Nothing remains from the first wooden
building, although fragments of pillars in the north aisle arcade are
from the earlier stone building. The bases of these pillars have
curious Norman carvings of the head of a bishop wearing a mitre.
St. Oswald, to whom the church is dedicated, was king of Nor-
thumbria, Winwick being his southernmost stronghold. It was
probably here that he was killed in the battle against King Penda of
Mercia.

The tower surmounted by a spire was built in 1358, re-building
and additions to the rest of the church being made in 1530–40 and
1701 when the fine roof to the nave was completed.

The cross arm of the Celtic wheelhead preaching cross to be seen
in the Gerard chapel is probably 1,000 years old. The old font is
14th century. In the floor of the chapel may be seen the rather badly
worn brass of 1495 to Peter Gerard. He is wearing armour, his feet
resting on a lion couchant. The Leigh Chantry chapel, dating from
1330, contains the brass of Peter Leigh, wearing armour of a knight
under the vestments of a priest. His wife lies beside him. The brass
is on the wall and bears the date 1527.

Brass rubbing at Winwick parish church

Bootle Museum
Oriel Road, Bootle. Route: A565 from Liverpool. Opening Times: Monday–Friday 9 a.m.–7 p.m.; Saturday 9 a.m.–1 p.m.; Closed Sunday.

BOOTLE Museum and Art Gallery is housed on the first floor of the town's central library building. Its permanent display contains the Lancaster Collection of English pottery and porcelain. Of particular interest is the Bishop Collection of Liverpool pottery. During the 17th century Liverpool was one of the main centres for the making of English Delft ware. This pottery takes its name from the Dutch town of Delft; the "Delft" process was popular in many countries, and in England pottery of this type was made at Bristol, Lambeth and Liverpool.

To make Delft the shaped earthenware was fired and then covered with a thick white enamel which contained oxide of tin. Designs were then painted on the white surface before a final lead glaze was applied and the article was fired for a second time. Blue design was used as this was almost the only colour which could be applied under a glaze and would withstand the heat of a second firing without changing colour. The process was a breakthrough in pottery design and manufacture since it provided a clear white background for decoration. It enabled pottery makers to use earthenware as a successful imitation of white china. Delft from different areas has its own characteristics. Liverpool Delft is noted for a bluish tinge in its glaze; it is tougher and more glassy than its Dutch counterpart.

Fletcher Moss Museum, Didsbury
The Old Parsonage, Didsbury. On the A34 Manchester–Cheadle road. Open May–August: Weekdays 10 a.m.–8 p.m.; Sundays 2.30 p.m.–8 p.m. September–April: Weekdays 10 a.m.–dusk; Sundays 2.30 p.m.–dusk.

THIS beautiful early Victorian house is set in attractive old fashioned gardens. For many years its was the much loved home of Mr. Fletcher Moss, alderman, magistrate and author of many books on local homes and history. On his death in 1919 Mr. Moss bequeathed the house and its garden to the Corporation of Manchester, in order that it should be kept as an example of a typical middle class English home. This aim has been adapted so that now the house.is used as a museum and art gallery, showing furniture and paintings. There are some fine water colour paintings and selected arrangements of furniture.

The Old Parsonage adjoins the old *Cock Inn*, which takes its name from the sport of cock fighting. For a time the house was connected with the local church and was inhabited by clergy. In the first half of the 19th century the untimely death of a curate's wife caused enough scandal to force the curate to flee the district. The house was presented to a new person who soon left it, saying that it was haunted.

A succession of tenants tried to live in the house but failed as the hauntings and reputation of the property grew worse. Finally, in 1865 Fletcher Moss went to live there with his parents. They found the ghosts harmless and inoffensive, and gradually the hauntings ceased and the ghosts faded away. The Old Parsonage is a charming example of a Victorian family house, and well worth a visit.

Monks Hall Museum, Eccles
42, Wellington Road, Swinton, Eccles. A57 from Manchester. Open Monday, Tuesday, Wednesday, Friday 10 a.m.–6 p.m.; Saturday 10 a.m.–5 p.m.

MONKS HALL was built in the 16th century, but was altered when additions were made at the beginning of the 19th century. It is an attractive building and the oldest secular property in Eccles. For three centuries it was used as a farmhouse, later becoming a private residence before the Corporation of Eccles bought it and adapted it in 1961 as a museum and art gallery.

The museum specialises in temporary exhibitions and presents displays of artistic, industrial and scientific interest. In addition to these there is a permanent collection of pictures, ceramics and Eccles bygones. Of special interest is an exhibition of work by James Nasmyth, the inventor of the steam hammer, who worked for some time at the local Bridgewater Foundry. There is a collection of machine tools and one of his steam hammers. The museum also shows an observation beehive and a series of monthly night sky charts.

Liverpool City Museums
Open: Monday–Saturday, 10 a.m.–5 p.m.; Sunday, 2 p.m.–5 p.m.

THE original museum, as designed by John Weightman, was a large and impressive building which was presented to the city in 1860 by William Brown, M.P. The foundation of the first collection came about through the generosity of the thirteenth Earl of Derby, and of Joseph Mayer, a Liverpool goldsmith. The Derby collection, as it is now known, comprised natural history exhibits and chief among these was a magnificent collection of birds. Joseph Mayer's first bequests to the museum were a collection of anthropological and archaeological specimens. He continued to augment the museum's treasures with additional collections of ivory, gold and jewellery, and fossils and plants. In later years the various collections increased to such an extent that housing them became a problem, and in 1906 was built an extra gallery known as the Horseshoe on account of its shape.

During the Second World War Liverpool's museum was totally wrecked by fire, and although much was lost the greater part of the material had fortunately been removed for safekeeping. Rebuilding did not begin until 1966 and the section that is at present open to the public contains some of the museum's most important exhibits. These include galleries dealing with prehistoric life, shipping, local history and the arts, plus the addition of an aquarium and new lecture theatres. At the present time the City Museums also hold exhibitions at Sudley House, in the Mosseley Hill district, bequeathed to the city by Miss Emma Holt. The second phase of the rebuilding programme is already well advanced and there are plans for including a transport section, an astronomy gallery and planetarium. Eventually it is hoped that a branch museum will be established at the Pier Head dealing exclusively with maritime exhibits.

Walker Art Gallery, Liverpool
Permanent Collection open: Monday–Saturday 10 a.m.–5 p.m.; Sunday 2 p.m.–5 p.m. In addition to the permanent collection several rooms are usually devoted to special exhibitions.

THE Walker Art Gallery was opened to the public in 1877. The first collection was started with paintings belonging to William Roscoe, a Liverpool lawyer and patron of the arts. Until his death in 1831 William Roscoe lived at Allerton Hall, now surrounded by Clarke Gardens, one of Liverpool's park areas. Additional purchases and bequests over the years have provided the gallery with a collection which is one of the finest in the country. Of particular note are: Simone Martini's "Christ discovered in the Temple", the famous painting entitled "And when did you last see your father?" and Ruben's "Virgin and child with St. Elizabeth and the child Baptist". The latter was acquired in 1960.

There are in existence some prints showing scenes of early Liverpool; one in particular is of a type of long legged wading bird feeding off the mud flats. It has been suggested that the mythical

Liver bird has some tenuous connections with these wading birds which were once common along the estuary of the river Mersey.

Heaton Hall, Manchester
Heaton Park, Manchester. Take the Bury Old Road out of Manchester. Open: May–August: Weekdays 10 a.m.–8 p.m.; Sundays 2 p.m.–8 p.m. September, October, March and April: Weekdays 10 a.m.–6 p.m.; Sundays 2 p.m.–6 p.m. November–February: Weekdays 10 a.m.– 4 p.m.; Sundays 2 p.m.–4 p.m.

HEATON HALL was designed in 1772 by James Wyatt and built for Sir Thomas Egerton. A most attractive building, it has retained much of its character and charm. The Hall is now used as a museum and art gallery, and is administered by the Corporation of Manchester. It makes a splendid setting for its exhibitions of 18th century paintings and silver. Little of the original furniture has survived, but special arrangements of selected 18th century furniture are shown.

Of special interest is the music room which contains a two-manual organ built in 1790 by Samuel Green. The organ is used three times a year when special concerts are held. Tickets for the concerts cost about $17\frac{1}{2}$p; for further details of dates and programmes contact the Museum Curator, Heaton Hall, Heaton Park.

Manchester Transport Museum
Heaton Park. Opening Times: Scheduled for opening 1971–2.

SOME years after Manchester Corporation discontinued their tram services it was decided to preserve a record of this form of transport. Heaton Park was chosen as the site and it is intended to open both the museum and a section of line during 1971–2. The static display will probably be housed in the old kitchens at Heaton Hall, and rolling stock will include a restored single deck tramcar (No. 765) and a small open top double deck car which dates from 1901. There are also plans for rebuilding a horse drawn tramcar of the type once used in Manchester. Service vehicles will be represented by two overhead tower wagons, one being of the horse drawn type and the other a petrol engined "Thorneycroft" of 1948.

It is proposed that a section of tram line would run between the Middleton Road entrance to Heaton Park and a terminal some 380 yards distant. From an historical viewpoint the opening of the tramway on this site would be of special significance since this was the point at which tramcars entered the park during their years of operation. Manchester Corporation practice in tramway operation would be followed in detail and all the equipment used would be authentic in character. A feeder box, "stop" and "stage" signs and other examples of street furniture as used on Manchester's tramways would be placed at appropriate positions along the route.

Educational visits by school parties could be arranged at any time to suit requirements. Precise details of opening times have not yet been decided upon, but it is likely that the museum will be open daily during the summer period. Estimated cost per tram ride is 5p.

Manchester Museum
The University, Oxford Road, Manchester. Open: Weekdays 10 a.m.–5 p.m.; Wednesdays 10 a.m.–9 p.m.

THE museum was formed 150 years ago through the activities of the Manchester Society of Natural History and still continues the tradition of presenting specialised exhibitions of natural and ancient history. There is a large and interesting collection of geological specimens, with displays of mineralogy and crystallography, and a special display of Blue John stones from Castleton, Derbyshire. There is a sectioned globe showing the internal structure of the earth, and a geological column showing the earth's main events in geological time. Of special interest is a collection of ancient rocks and fossils, including a fossil forest of the Carboniferous period. There is a large zoological section in the museum, showing mammals, birds, fish and reptiles, with a display of insects showing those both helpful and harmful to man. The botany collection shows the main plant groupings, with their natural uses and diversifications.

The museum has departments of ethnology and numismatics, and a large and extremely fine display of Egyptian antiquities. Outside the British Museum department of Egyptology, this is one of the best displays of its kind in the country. Show cases are illustrated to depict the everyday life of ancient Egypt as lived by ordinary people. There are several mummies and a furnished funeral chamber in the "Tomb of the Two Brothers." There is a good display of pottery, inscribed stones and tools, with an exhibition of the techniques involved in Egyptian weaving and the writing of hieroglyphics. There is an extensive reserve collection to this department. For permission to view, a written application should be made to the Keeper of the Egyptology Department.

The museum will provide a fascinating outing for all members of the family. Specially for children, there is a museum club which meets on Saturday mornings, and on some Wednesday mornings during school holidays. The club is supervised by teachers from the museum school department, and children are encouraged to discover and record interesting facts about museum exhibits.

Platt Hall, Manchester: Gallery of English Costume

*Route: A34, two miles south of Manchester. Opening Times: Week-
days May–October 10 a.m.–8 p.m.; November–February 10 a.m.–4
p.m.; March–April 10 a.m.–6 p.m. Sunday 2 p.m. to above closing
times.*

EARLY in the 17th century the Platt estate came into the possession
of the Worsley family and the first owner, Ralph Worsley, gave
land for the building of Platt chapel. His son Charles became
prominent as one of Cromwell's major generals at the time of the
Commonwealth. Deborah Worsley inherited the property after the
death of her brother in 1759, and it was her husband John Lees
who commissioned the building of the new house. Platt Hall was
completed in 1764 and several sets of plans and drawings by different
architects are now on exhibition. Also in 1764 the painter Richard
Wilson was commissioned by the family, and his work "River View"
is once again hanging in its original position at Platt Hall, having
been bought back for the city by Manchester Art Gallery. Deborah
and John Lees had no children, but Thomas who was a son by a
former marriage was adopted and took the name Carill-Worsley.
This family name can be traced through to the last private owner
who sold Platt Hall to Manchester Corporation in 1907.

As recently as 1954 Platt Hall received from Mrs. Tindal-Carill-
Worsley a trunk full of 18th century garments which had belonged
to her great-grandfather, Thomas Carill-Worsley. This gift formed
the nucleus around which the costume museum has been built, and
among the items in the trunk were corded silk suits, embroidered

71|11067

Old costumes at Platt Hall Art Gallery

waistcoats and two hats showing the fashion for "cocking" or three-cornered brims. Also included was Thomas' monogrammed walking stick, and dresses and muffs belonging to his wife Elizabeth. The Platt Hall Costume Gallery now ranks as one of the most comprehensive collections of English clothing and features items representative of every fashion era up to the 1920s.

For the benefit of those interested in the study of English costume the Gallery has published a number of illustrated books and a wide range of post-cards and colour transparencies. Address enquiries to: Manchester City Art Gallery, Mosley Street, Manchester M2 3JL.

Manchester Museum of Science and Technology
Grosvenor Street, Manchester. Open: Monday–Friday 10 a.m.–5 p.m.

THE museum displays some of the main scientific and industrial inventions made in the North West of England. On the ground floor of the museum different types of powered machinery are displayed. There are examples of engines driven by steam, hot air, gas and petrol, with a third scale model of Thomas Newcomen's first steam engine of 1712. The development of the internal combustion engine is shown with the Otto Atmospheric Gas engine of 1869, which was the forerunner of the engine from which today's motor car engines are directly descended. Also shown is Royce's second motor car engine, which led to the formation of the Rolls Royce partnership.

On the first floor are examples of spinning wheels, looms, cloth printing machines and textiles. Richard Arkwright's water-frame, the machine he patented in 1769 for the spinning of cotton, is shown here. On the top floor of the museum the work of famous Manchester scientists is illustrated. It includes Priestley, who discovered oxygen, and John Dalton who devised a theory of atomic elements and weights. It displays some of the apparatus used by James Joule, who determined the mechanical equivalent of heat.

The museum also exhibits part of the National Paper Museum, showing how paper was made by hand. There is a lecture room at the museum, and talks and demonstrations can be given for schools or other parties, if written application is made beforehand.

Salford Museum and Art Gallery
Peel Park, Salford, 5. Open: April–September: Weekdays 10 a.m.–6 p.m.; Sundays 2–5 p.m. October–March: Weekdays 10 a.m.–5 p.m.; Sundays 2–5 p.m. Closed Christmas Day, Boxing Day, New Year's Day and Good Friday.

SALFORD MUSEUM stands on the site of Lark Hill Mansion, erected in the early 1790s and demolished in 1937 when the present buildings were constructed. It contains a most interesting display of

"Lark Hill Place," Salford Museum and Art Gallery

British folk life material, and its collection of social and domestic items is one of the largest in the North-West. Inside the museum the buildings known as "Lark Hill Place" were constructed to show a full scale reproduction of shops and houses from the past life of Salford, ranging from the 17th to 19th centuries, with furnishing of the period. This is a fascinating street scene, full of detail and interest for anyone keen to recapture the atmosphere of yesterday's world. Domestic bygones, curios, furnishings and fashions are all shown in their everyday authentic settings.

The 17th century two-storey merchant's house has panelled walls, and a portrait of Sir Robert Honewood and his wife, 1630, is painted on them. Some 17th century utensils are to be seen in the room. The public house of Lark Hill Place is the *Blue Lion Tavern*, typical of those built in Salford at the end of the 19th century with its spittoons and sawdust on the floor. Opposite we see the chemist and druggist; large glass carboys filled with coloured water are in the window, and inside such things as were used by Florence Nightingale in the Crimean war of 1854—a tongue scraper, face-ache pills and Balsamic plaster—are to be found on the shelves.

There is a two-roomed cottage with a single living-room on the ground floor for all cooking, washing and eating, with a single bedroom above reached by a plank ladder. On the table, places have been laid for a meal. Further on is a typical late Victorian house. Over one of the windows is fixed a metal plaque, known as a fire mark. The house is completely furnished in the style of the period. Grace and elegance is shown in the Georgian house which may well have been modelled on the original Lark Hill mansion.

In the forge is a 200lb. anvil together with all the tools of the blacksmith and wheelwright. The bow-windows of the dressmakers display the fashions of the last century, frequently changed to show the transformations that took place between the Regency and Edwardian eras.

Among all the other shops perhaps the one most likely to appeal to younger members of the family is the toy shop with its lovely dapple grey rocking horse, doll's pram with cane wheels and Noah's Ark. There is an old toy steam engine and an array of "tin" soldiers marching to battle in 1870. The street also contains a "Victoria" carriage, a "Brougham," a "Boneshaker" bicycle and a "Penny-farthing," as well as the pole used by a knocker-up and a lamplighter's stick.

The museum also houses the town's Art Gallery. This shows frequent exhibitions of works by Northern artists, all of a high standard. The gallery's permanent collection is noted for its display of pictures by L. S. Lowry. His studies of the northern industrial and social scene are famous and have won him international acclaim. He specialises in depicting the poorer areas, and has painted many street scenes of Salford and Manchester.

Salford Science Museum
Buile Hill Park, Pendleton, Salford 6. Open: April–September:
Weekdays 10 a.m.–6 p.m.; Sundays 2 p.m.–5 p.m. October–March:
Weekdays 10 a.m.–5 p.m.; Sundays 2 p.m.–5 p.m. Closed Christmas
Day, Boxing Day, New Year's Day and Good Friday.

THE museum specialises in showing the history, techniques and
apparatus of coal mining, and possesses an extremely good model
coal mine, "Buile Hill No. 1 Pit." The pit is a full reproduction of
coal workings, and shows the methods that have been used in coal
mining from the early 19th century to the present day. These early
pits were often highly dangerous, the coal industry was expanding
rapidly and miners were encouraged to dig deeper and further afield
in search of coal. One of their greatest dangers was "firedamp" gas,
which was highly explosive. The model shows how Davy lamps were
used to light the mine tunnels and combat the danger of explosions,
and how safety fuses were applied to gunpowder blasting. The
visitor can follow the progress in mining methods from the picks
and hand drill of the last century to the modern coal cutting machines
and compressed air drills of today.

From April to September guided parties of not more than 15
people are taken round the pit three times a day (Sundays excluded)
at 2.30, 3.30 and 4.30 p.m. Tours are free of charge, and tickets for
them are obtained on request at the desk in the museum entrance
hall.

The other collections in the museum are mainly associated with
the exhibitions in the model coal mines. There is a display of early
mining equipment which is contrasted with some of the latest
apparatus to be used—including self advancing pit props and a
rocker shovel. There is a description of the Lancashire coal field,
covering the formation of coal and coal fossils. The museum also
presents items of local natural history, and shows a collection of
British and foreign animals and birds.

The Pilkington Glass Museum, St. Helens
Prescot Road, St. Helens. On A57 Liverpool–St. Helens road. Open:
Weekdays 10 a.m.–5 p.m. (Wednesdays until 9 p.m.); Weekends and
Bank Holidays 2 p.m.–4.30 p.m. All visits must be confirmed by the
Museum secretary, Tel. St. Helens 28882 extension 2499.

THE museum was first planned as a visual history of Pilkington's
glass factory for the people of St. Helens. Since then it has
developed into the most complete historical record of glass making
techniques in the world. It is a most interesting museum, and one
well worth a visit. The first glass makers in Lancashire were the
Romans, who used the natural supplies of wood as their fuel. It
was centuries later that new manufacturers moved their factories to

St. Helens to be near the source of coal. Since the 18th century St. Helens has been one of the main centres of glass making in the world. Plate glass was manufactured here in 1773 and at Ravenhead the original glass house—known as "The Cathedral"—is still in use.

The Glass Museum illustrates the story of glass making from the time of the Ancient Egyptians to the present day. Displays show the many uses of glass through the ages, with all the different techniques involved in its manufacture. There is a history of English window glass from the 16th century, with an exhibition of the many types of industrial and stained glass. There are displays of ancient and foreign glass, including one showing the 200 year old technique of making Venetian goblets. A film is shown to visitors twice daily, at 10 a.m. and 3.15 p.m. in the museum cinema on the ground floor.

7

Docks and Waterways

The Port of Liverpool

OVER the span of five centuries Liverpool has changed from a little fishing village into one of Europe's leading ports. Liverpool was granted its charter as a seaport by King John in 1207 and from then onwards the variety of goods and raw materials handled has reflected the changing trade patterns of the British Isles. The importing of sugar from the West Indies, and cotton and tobacco from America, plus the exporting of Lancashire's textiles after the Industrial Revolution all served to increase the tonnage handled at Liverpool docks. The gradual silting up of the river Dee provided an obvious increase in the importance of the Mersey estuary, and by the 18th century Liverpool led the world in its construction of the first modern deep water docks.

Today there are seven miles of docks, 37 miles of quays and Liverpool can claim ownership of another unique feature, the Landing Stage, which is the largest floating structure in the world. Along its impressive length there are facilities for anything from an ocean liner to a small ferry boat. Plans for the provision of a further fourteen deep water berths are already under way at an estimated cost of £36 million. Of the 25,300,000 tons of cargo handled annually the bulk consists of: iron and steel, ore, oil and petroleum, vehicles and machinery, chemicals and textiles, salt, sugar, fruit and grain, cotton and wood. The traffic of Liverpool docks is watched over by the Liver birds who perch atop the Royal Liver Building and who seem to have become the symbol of Liverpool. The Liver bird is probably one of Liverpool's most renowned citizens, and it is traditionally accepted that the city takes its name from this mythical bird.

Visits to Gladstone Dock can be arranged for parties of school children by application to the Information Officer, Mersey Docks and Harbour Board, Pier House, Liverpool.

The Port of Manchester

The Ship Canal. The port of Manchester is unique, for although

Liner sailing from Manchester docks to Canada

50 miles from the open sea it has become Britain's third port. To the Manchester city centre come ocean-going ships from all over the world. For the final stage of their journey they travel by a man-made ship canal nearly 36 miles long.

Some 250 years ago, when spinning and weaving began to flourish in the Lancashire area, communications to the outside world hardly existed. Travelling westwards towards the coast it was only possible to go as far as Warrington with a wagon and horses; to proceed any further meant resorting to pack-horses, or barges along devious river routes. As industry developed it became readily apparent that communications between Manchester and Liverpool would have to be improved. Initially work was done to make the river Mersey navigable as far as Warrington. In 1714 an application was made for an Act "for making the rivers Mersey and Irwell navigable from Liverpool to Manchester," but it was 1720 before the Act was passed.

In 1761 the Duke of Bridgewater opened the first and second sections of his Bridgewater Canal to carry coal from his collieries at Worsley into the heart of Manchester, and thereby cutting his transport costs by half. Anxious to add to this success the Duke proceeded next with a canal link to Liverpool, which not only carried his coal but provided the vital outlet to the sea that Lancashire industry required for its products to reach the markets of the world. Instead of bringing prosperity to both towns the port of Liverpool took advantage of its position and monopoly, and Manchester found its new prosperity wilting visibly. The proposals of the past for a ship canal to be built to Manchester were now re-examined and considered seriously; the proposals went before Parliament in December 1882, and after three years of bitter struggle were finally passed in 1885. Construction of the canal with its five locks involved up to 17,000 navvies, 80 steam excavators and land dredgers, and cost £15 million. It was finally completed on January 1st, 1894, after many setbacks and difficulties.

The Docks. The Terminal Docks at Salford are impressive, with the half-mile long No. 9 Dock, the 40,000 ton capacity grain elevator and the vast South 6 transit shed with extensive timber-handling facilities. At Eastham, where the canal joins the river Mersey, there is the superb Queen Elizabeth II Dock. Opened in 1954 it is the largest dock in Britain and can handle four tankers of 32,000 tons dead weight. Pipelines take the fuel up the side of the canal to the tank farm at Stanlow, around which most major oil companies have installations. At Ellesmere Port and Runcorn there are also impressive handling facilities. For the visitor one of the most interesting features on the canal is the Barton Swing Aqueduct. This is a swing bridge which carries a narrow boat canal over the ship canal. To allow the big ships to continue their passage the bridge is swung full of water.

Up the canal comes petroleum, grain, timber, cotton and foodstuffs. Down it go iron and steel, chemicals and a variety of manufactured goods—machinery, vehicles, and textile fibres. In all approximately 5,000 ships carrying over 16,750,000 tons of goods enter the port of Manchester each year.

Tours of the Docks. Tours arranged by the public relations department of the port of Manchester consist of a visit to he principal points of interest on the docks followed by a water tour on the company's water-bus of the upper reaches of the waterway, from the Terminal Docks at Manchester to the Barton Aqueduct and return. Duration of the tours is approximately two hours. Tours may be arranged for parties not exceeding 50 in number. Small groups and individuals are joined to existing parties when vacancies occur. Special application must be made for children under the age of 9 years, who must be accompanied by adults.

Applications for bookings should be made to the Public Relations Department, the Port of Manchester, Ship Canal House, King Street, Manchester M2 4WX. Telephone 061–832 2244. Telephone bookings must be confirmed within 7 days. Envelopes should be marked TOURS in the top left-hand corner. Tours are available from mid-February to 30 November, commencing at 10.30 a.m. and 2.30 p.m. Monday to Saturday. A charge of 10p is made, payable in advance. Permits are required for cameras. Full-length tours from Manchester to Liverpool are arranged by Co-operative Travel Service, 1 Balloon Street, Manchester M60 4ES, Telephone 061–834 1212, to whom application should be made for further particulars.

8

Sports and Hobbies

IN this section it has only been possible to give the names and addresses of a few of the more specialised clubs. Those requiring information on other clubs and societies in local areas should apply to their Town Hall or Public Library where a comprehensive list will be found.

Aero Clubs

THE Lancashire Aero Club has its headquarters at Barton Aerodrome, Eccles. The club has a fleet of six aircraft, use of the control tower, and a pleasant club house. Members are given individual instruction by fully qualified flying instructors, and for those already holding a private pilot's licence there is the opportunity of instruction in instrument flying, night flying, and the use of advanced radio aids to navigation. Flying lessons can be booked and flying is every day from 10 a.m. to sunset, weather permitting.

The cost of membership is £2.10 entrance fee, and £9.45 annual subscription. The entrance fee is waived for members' wives and children under the age of 21, and the annual subscription is £3.15. For further details please write to the Lancashire Aero Club, Barton Aerodrome, Eccles. Tel. Eccles 1866.

The Southport and Merseyside Aero Club headquarters are at Liverpool Airport. Aircraft are available for hire and instruction can be given if required.

Angling

IT is usually possible to obtain day tickets to fish from the many piers that abound on the Lancashire coast line. For those who prefer a more specialised type of angling it is often possible to obtain day tickets or weekly permits to fish in one of the rivers or reservoirs. As the names and addresses of local secretaries are liable to change, those interested should obtain a complete and up to date list from the Lancashire River Authority, 48 West Cliff, Preston, telephone number Preston 54921.

Archery.

ORIGINALLY a means of hunting and war, archery has been considered a sport for many hundreds of years. The Royal Company of Archers was founded in 1676. In Lancashire there are many archery clubs both for field and target archery, the oldest club dating back to 1902. This is the Bowmen of Pendle and Samlesbury who shoot in the grounds of Samlesbury Hall. Other clubs include the Blackpool Bowmen, Billinge Bowmen (near Wigan), the Bowmen of Overdale, the Grange and Allithwaite Archers, Mersey Bowmen, Preston Archers and the Walverden Bowmen. Further information may be obtained by writing to the Secretary of the Grand National Archery Society, 20, Broomfield Road, Chelmsford, Essex.

Canoeing.

THERE are a number of local canoe clubs in Lancashire affiliated to the British Canoe Union, these including the Manchester Canoe Club, the Grappenhall Athletic Canoe Club, the Lakeland Canoe Club and the Canoe Camping Club. Membership of the B.C.U. is 75p per year for a full member, and further details may be obtained from the General Secretary, British Canoe Union, 26/29 Park Crescent, London, W.1. The canoe clubs in Lancashire arrange many events, both inside and outside the county, and these include slaloms, sea surfing, cruises, regattas and wild water races. Meetings are held on stretches of the Dee, Lune, Ribble, Wharfe and other Pennine rivers.

Folk Dancing.

THE English Folk Dance and Song Society (North Lancashire District) both organise and take part in many interesting events throughout the county. These include barn dances, folk dance parties and social events during the winter months, and displays at carnivals and processions during the summer. The Leyland Morris Men undertake evening tours of the local towns and villages, sometimes accompanied by the Furness Morris Men and the Hoghton Rapper Sword Team. The Manchester Morris Men specialise in the traditional clog processional dances of this region. Further details of the many local clubs and events may be obtained by writing to the Area Organiser, 4 Bluecoat Chambers, School Lane, Liverpool 1.

Go-karting.

THE Lancashire Kart Club organise monthly meetings at Burton-wood, near Warrington, throughout the year. Membership of the club is £1.50 per year, and for juniors 75p. The club is R.A.C. approved, and members can compete at any R.A.C. circuit in the U.K. or in any international event held abroad. Other clubs in Lancashire include the Ribble Kart Club which meets at Flookburgh (near Grange-over-Sands); the Morecambe and Heysham Kart Club which meets at Heysham Head; and the Lion Kart Club which organises events at Tern Hill.

Sub Aqua Clubs.

THE British Sub Aqua Club has many local branches throughout Lancashire, the addresses of which can be obtained from the headquarters of the club at 25 Orchard Road, Kingston-upon-Thames, Surrey. Inland as well as coastal towns are represented and, although most of the diving is done in the sea and lakes, many clubs have "practice nights" at their local swimming baths. Included among the activities of sub aqua enthusiasts are such programmes as: (a) underwater surveys for different biological, archaeological and fishing societies; (b) searches for sunken boats and wrecks; (c) lobster and crab fishing. Organised parties of B.S.A.C. members travel to diving locations in various parts of the British Isles.

Vintage Cars

THERE is a growing interest in Lancashire in vintage cars, and many events are held which are of interest to practically every-one. The Manchester Vintage Car Club has a membership of over eighty. A monthly meeting is held at the *Bulls Head*, Hale Barns, on the first Monday of each month throughout the year. The club's summer calendar includes many road events, the highlight being the annual driving tests which are held in May. The club is associated with the Preston and District Vintage Car Club. Further details of the Manchester Vintage Car Club may be obtained by writing to the Secretary, The Spinney, 1 Copperfield Road, Cheadle, Cheshire.

Affiliated Clubs of the Royal Yachting Association
South

Locality:	*Club:*
Blundlesands, Nr. Formby	Blundlesands Sailing Club
Chew Valley, Greenfield, Nr. Mossley	Dovestone Sailing Club
The Flash, Lowton St. Marys	Leigh Sailing Club
Pennington Flash, Nr. Leigh	Lowton Sailing Club
Leigh Flash	Manchester University Yacht Club
Leigh	Manchester University Womens Yacht Club
Liverpool Speke	Liverpool Sailing Club
Manchester	Manchester Cruising Club
	Worsley Cruising Club
Southport Marine Lake	West Lancashire Yacht Club
	Southport Sailing Club
	Liverpool University Sailing Club
St. Helens, Eccleston Mere	Pilkington Sailing Club
Warrington, Penketh	Fidlers Ferry Sailing Club
Upper Gorton Reservoir, Manchester	Fairfield Golf and Sailing Club

Events

FEBRUARY

Liverpool:

The Liverpool Antique Fair is held for four days at the Bluecoat Chambers, School Lane, Liverpool. A number of exhibitors have individual stands where they display antique furniture, silver, china, glass and paintings. All the exhibits are for sale. A large number of other events are held at the Bluecoat Chambers, including recitals, concerts, painting exhibitions, evenings of contemporary music and jazz.

Manchester:

The Northern Camping and Caravan Show is held at Belle Vue. The Show lasts for one week and is in the Lancaster and Central Halls. Times of opening are: Saturday and Sunday, 10 a.m.–9 p.m. Weekdays, 2.0 p.m.–9 p.m.

A large number of shows and exhibitions are held each year at Belle Vue, in addition to the many permanent attractions. Of the latter, the zoo includes an aquarium and reptilium, open enclosures for lions and tigers, wolves, apes, bear pits, and a children's zoo. There is also a fun fair, a scenic railway, veteran car ride, performing sea lions, and a model village. Belle Vue is open daily at 10 a.m. Admission charges are 20p for adults, 10p for children.

MARCH

Liverpool:

An annual concert is given by the Youth Orchestra at the Philharmonic Hall. For further details please write to the Philharmonic Hall, Box Office, Hope Street, Liverpool, L1 9BP.

Manchester:

A choral and orchestral concert is given by the Northern School of Music at the Free Trade Hall. For further details please write to the Free Trade Hall, Peter Street, Manchester 2.

The Manchester Championship two-day dog show is held in the Exhibition Hall, Belle Vue. Open from 7 a.m.–8 p.m.

There is speedway racing at Belle Vue, Manchester, each Saturday

evening from March to October. Racing commences at 7.0 p.m.
The British League Riders' Championship takes place in October.
Stock car racing is also held at Belle Vue.

APRIL

Manchester:

The three day Manchester Flower Show is held at the Showground,
Platt Field Park, Manchester.

Middleton:

A mummers' play is performed in Middleton on Easter Monday.
This play has recently been revived by a group of local people.

St. Helens:

Sportsboat racing, inboard and outboard, is held regularly at
Carr Mill from April to September. Admission is $12\frac{1}{2}$p, car park free.
Access is via gateway in Carr Mill Road. The races are organised by
the Lancashire Powerboat Racing Club. Raceday practice is usually
from 11 a.m. and racing begins at 2 p.m.

MAY

Manchester:

An annual toy fair is held in the Lancaster Hall, Belle Vue. This
is a five day Show. Times of opening are: Sunday, 10 a.m.–5 p.m.
Monday and Tuesday, 10 a.m.–6 p.m. Wednesday, 10 a.m.–9 p.m.
Thursday, 10 a.m.–3 p.m.

A one day Spring Brass Band Festival is held in the Kings Hall
and Exhibition Halls at Belle Vue.

At the Free Trade Hall, Peter Street, Manchester, a Scots night
with Scottish singers, a pipe band and Scottish country dancing is
held.

On the first Saturday in May the Manchester Morris Men join
with the Manchester District of the English Folk Dance and Song
Society to dance a tour of the city. The Manchester Morris Men,
who specialise in longsword, rapper sword and Cotswold dances,
dance at the many charity carnivals held in the local Manchester
boroughs. These includes Flixton, Droylsden, Failsworth and
Castleton.

An annual driving test is held by the Manchester Vintage Car Club.
(See under Sports and Hobbies page 61).

The two annual Whit Walks which take place in Manchester
have a deeply religious significance. The Church of England procession, which for the last two years has taken place on Spring Bank
Holiday Monday, dates back to 1801. The procession consists of
children from all the Sunday Schools who walk through the streets
to a service at the Cathedral. The Roman Catholic procession is
believed to be linked to the sudden large increase of Catholics in

Manchester by the Irish immigrants about the year 1843. This procession has taken place on Whit Sunday for the past two years.
Warrington:
The Walton Horse Show is held on Spring Bank Holiday Monday.

JUNE

Liverpool:
An annual exhibition of work is held at the Bluecoat Chambers, School Lane, Liverpool, by the Painters and Sculptors Group.
Manchester:
During the months of June and July, two weeks of popular concerts are presented at the Free Trade Hall by the Halle Orchestra. Full details may be obtained from the Halle Booking Office, 11 Cross Street, Manchester, M2 1WE.

An open day and horse show is held at Wythenshaw Park, usually in early June. This is a one day event. There is no charge for admission and refreshments are available.

A one day show is held in Heaton Park in mid-June. Admission is free. It includes a horse show, gymkhana, and morris dancing competitions. Further details of these two shows may be obtained by writing to the Director, City of Manchester Parks Department, Cumberland House, Crown Square, Manchester.

Manchester to Blackpool Road Walk: A road race attracting a large number of competitors.

Manchester to Blackpool Veteran and Vintage Car Run: This very popular event finishes with a rally at Stanley Park, Blackpool.
Oldham:
The Oldham Corporation horse show is a one day event at Alexandra Park.

JULY

Aintree:
On the Club circuit at Aintree, races for both motor cycles and motor cars take place, though the Grand Prix circuit is now closed.
Formby:
A one day horticultural and agricultural show is held each year in Duke Street Park, Formby. This is said to be one of the finest one day shows in the country, and attracts a large number of visitors.
Liverpool:
A three day agricultural and horticultural show is held at Wavertree, Liverpool. This large show attracts competitors from all over the country and includes many interesting displays in addition to the summer flower show, horses and cattle, small livestock shows, etc.

On July 12th Orangemen celebrate the victory of the Boyne.

Manchester:

An annual flower and horse shows takes place for three days at Platt Fields Park in late July.

St. Helens:

A three day agricultural show is held by the Corporation in Sherdley Park, St. Helens, usually during the third week in July.

Warrington:

The Lancashire Traction Engine Club annual rally is held at the Burtonwood Airfield. This is a two day rally, including steam engines, road locomotives and steam tractors. Also on view are veteran and vintage cars, motor cycles and historic commercial vehicles.

The Friday nearest July 1st is a public holiday. This is Warrington's Walking Day when congregations of churches of all denominations walk in procession through the town.

AUGUST

Kirkby:

The Kirkby Agricultural Society have a one day show at the showground, Central Recreation Ground, Cherryfield Drive, Kirkby, Liverpool.

Newton-le-Willows:

An annual town show is held on the third Saturday in August. The main features are a gymkhana, horticultural displays and various other competitions.

Oldham:

The one day Oldham Corporation sheepdog trial takes place in Alexandra Park, Oldham, commencing at 10.0 a.m. Other events include a donkey show, rabbit show, brass bands, athletic road race etc. Admission is free to all events with the exception of the rabbit show and the cage bird show.

Woolton:

The one day Woolton show is held at Camp Hill, Hillfoot Road, Woolton, and opens at 10.0 a.m. It includes show jumping, horses and cattle, dog show, flower show and morris dancing. There are also special children's entertainments.

SEPTEMBER

Manchester:

The annual British Open Brass Band Contest is held in the Kings Hall, Belle Vue, for one day from 11 a.m. to 5 p.m.

Liverpool:

Three series of concerts are held at the Royal Philharmonic Hall from September to May. The Tuesday Subscription Series (16 concerts) are fortnightly. Tickets are available from 12th August for Series tickets, 18th August for single tickets, 16th November for single tickets for the following year. The Week-end Series (16 concerts) are also fortnightly. Tickets are available as above. The Industrial Concerts are nine groups of monthly concerts with three identical concerts in each group. A concert syllabus is available, price 15p, from the Philharmonic Hall, Box Office, Hope Street, Liverpool, L1 9BP.

OCTOBER

Liverpool:
A folk music festival is held during October at the Bluecoat Chambers, School Lane.

A model railway and tram exhibition is staged every two years by the Merseyside Model Railway Society in conjunction with one of the Liverpool newspapers. It is a four day exhibition and includes working model railways and model tramcars. The next exhibition will be in 1972, and will be at the Bluecoat Chambers. Admission prices are: 15p for adults, 7½p for children.

Manchester:
The Northern Aquarists Exhibition is held in the Lancaster Hall, Belle Vue. This is a two day show, and exhibits from all over Lancashire are presented in special exhibition tanks. Most of the towns in Lancashire hold aquatic shows and exhibitions, but at the majority of these the fish are displayed in plain glass jars, as opposed to the special tanks here.

Between October and May various series of concerts are presented at the Free Trade Hall by the Halle Orchestra. These include: Thursday Series—a fortnightly series of 16 concerts; Sunday Series— a series of 16 concerts; Industrial Series—6 concerts presented on Wednesday and repeated on Thursday between October and May. A prospectus giving full details of these concerts may be obtained by writing to the Halle Booking Office, 11 Cross Street, Manchester, M2 1WE.

NOVEMBER

Manchester:
The Halle Choir perform choral works with the Halle Orchestra between November and May. The programme includes two carol concerts held during December. Further details may be obtained by writing to the Choir Secretary, Halle Concerts Society, 30 Cross Street, Manchester.

St. Helens:
A chrysanthemum and arts and crafts show is held at the Town Hall, St. Helens. This is a two day show.

DECEMBER

Formby:

At the Holy Trinity Church, Formby, on the Sunday before Christmas, children carry garlands of evergreen. They wait for the words, "Let the church be wreathed," and the garlands are placed within the church. This ceremony takes place during the afternoon.

Liverpool:

Carol concerts are held on four evenings during December, at the Royal Philharmonic Hall. Postal bookings from 2nd November; personal applications from 16th November. "The Messiah" (Handel) is held on two evenings after Christmas. Booking as above. Applications should be made to the Royal Philharmonic Hall, Box Office, Hope Street, Liverpool.

Manchester:

At Belle Vue an annual international circus is held from December to February in the Kings Hall. There are two performances on weekdays, except for Monday (one performance) and Saturday (four performances). For further details please write to the Publicity Department, Belle Vue (Manchester) Ltd., Belle Vue, Manchester 12.

The Halle Choir present "The Messiah" (Handel) at Belle Vue. Details may be obtained from the Halle Booking Office, 11 Cross Street, Manchester.

The Piccadilly Gardens are illuminated for the Christmas season.

KEY TO MAPS:

A 1. Burscough Priory
   2. Halsall Church
   3. Ormskirk Church
   4. Sefton Church
   5. Bootle Museum
B. 1. Middleton Church
   2. Heaton Hall
   3. Ashton-under-Lyne Church
C. 1. Eccles Museum
   2. Ordsall Hall, Salford
      Salford Museum
      Salford Science Museum
   3. Flixton Church
   4. Wythenshawe Hall
   5. Platt Hall
   6. Fletcher Moss, Didsbury
   7. Airport
D. 1. Billinge Church
   2. Winwick Church

   3. Pilkington Glass, St. Helens
   4. Huyton Church
   5. Childwall Church
   6. Speke Hall, Liverpool
E. LIVERPOOL
   1. Art Gallery
   2. Museum
   3. Metropolitan Cathedral
   4. Anglican Cathedral
   5. Tunnel entrances
   6. Albert Dock
   7. Waterfront (Pier Head)
F. MANCHESTER
   1. Cathedral
   2. Chetham School
   3. Town Hall
   4. John Rylands Library
   5. Manchester Museum

MAPS:

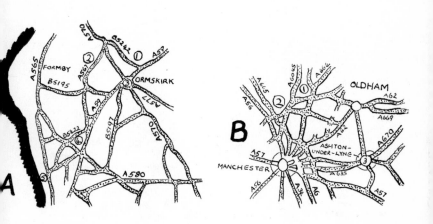

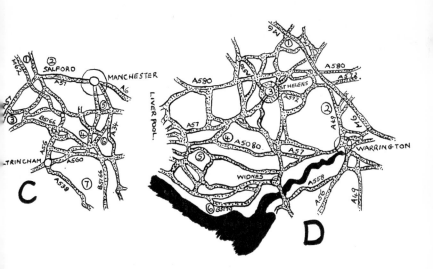

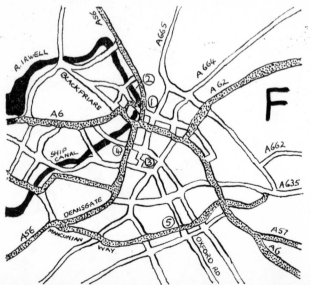

Index:

Index *(continued)*